| DATE | | | |
|------|--|--|--|
| JUL 16 '81 | | | |
| AUG 15 '85 | | | |
|  | | | |
|  | | | |
|  | | | |
|  | | | |
|  | | | |
|  | | | |
|  | | | |
|  | | | |
|  | | | |
|  | | | |
|  | | | |

# TIBET AND THE TIBETANS

# TIBET AN

*With Sixty-seven Illustrations and Two Maps*

*Foreword by George E. Taylor*

# IE TIBETANS

BY *Tsung-Lien Shen* 沈宗濂

AND *Shen-Chi Liu* 柳陞祺

## OCTAGON BOOKS

A DIVISION OF FARRAR, STRAUS AND GIROUX

New York   1973

*Reprinted 1973*
*by special arrangement with Stanford University Press*

OCTAGON BOOKS

A Division of Farrar, Straus & Giroux, Inc.
19 Union Square West
New York, N. Y. 10003

Library of Congress Cataloging in Publication Data

Shên, Tsung-lien.
    Tibet and the Tibetans.

    Reprint of the ed. published by Stanford University Press,
    Stanford, Calif.

    Bibliography: p.
    1. Tibet—History.   2. Tibet—Social life and customs.   I. Liu,
    Shêng-chi, joint author.   II. Title.
[DS786.S524   1973]                      915.15′03′5                      73-7735
ISBN 0-374-97310-5

# *Foreword*

The book by Mr. Tsung-lien Shen is important for at least two reasons. In the first place, it is the last statement on pre-Communist Tibet that we are likely to get. In the second place, it is the first book to deal with certain aspects of Tibet previously overlooked or not adequately covered.

Mr. Shen was a Chinese scholar of some standing before the circumstances of the last World War led to his appointment as resident Chinese Commissioner in Lhasa. While acquainted with Tibetan affairs before he went to his assignment, Mr. Shen began immediately on arrival a study of Tibetan civilization and institutions. He fell in love both with Tibetans and Tibet, and his book is in many ways a strong plea—now somewhat academic—to permit the Tibetans to run their own affairs. He most certainly considers them capable of self-government.

Mr. Shen did not learn the Tibetan language, but he had plenty of resident Chinese available as interpreters. His experiences are confined mainly to Lhasa and the surrounding area including the three big monasteries. Hence, the reader will not learn a great deal about the rest of Tibet. As Mr. Shen's association was confined largely to the upper classes, he does not pretend to offer much information about the farmers or the herders. His book provides, however, very important new data on city life, on the ruling class, on government, the church, and the monasteries. The chapter on the yearly cycle in Lhasa is an excellent device to give the reader a feeling for the rhythm of life in the capital and of the country as a whole, at least as far as it is reflected in the capital.

Mr. Shen is at his best where he goes into research that grows out of his own position as official representative of China. His official duties involved considerable dealings with the Tibetan authorities because he was charged with the mission to strengthen the ties between China and Tibet, and to keep open the cavaran route over which flowed a small but important amount of material to war-torn China. His description of government organization and bureaucracy contains much that is new, and the total picture is certainly much clearer than in most other sources. This is undoubtedly the most important contribution of his book. Aside from giving a vivid picture of the different branches of the government in action, he helps the reader to understand that even though the church controls the state the two are separate entities, and that, for an understanding of Tibetan politics, the state must not be over-looked. In his comments on religion, he deals most ably with the church and monastery organization.

In writing this book, Mr. Shen had the able assistance of a well-known Chinese scholar, Mr. Shen-chi Liu. Mr. Liu went to Tibet as Mr. Shen's secretary and stayed on there two years after Mr. Shen's departure in 1947. He collaborated in the research and is responsible for information on the more recent developments in Tibet. He is an excellent Tibetan scholar.

Based as it is on several years of residence in Tibet by men who were in a key position for observation and who made exceptionally good use of their opportunities, this book is an important addition to our knowledge of a comparatively unknown country.

GEORGE E. TAYLOR

Far Eastern and Russian Institute
University of Washington
February 2, 1952

# Preface

Tibet, since before its name was known to the world, has been the subject of the most extravagant stories as from the myth of the gold-digging ants of twenty-four centuries ago down to the modern fiction of Shangri-La.

The overwhelming majority are travelers' accounts which, though they include some fine literature, contain scrappy information gathered in trips hastily or more commonly stealthily taken. Only a small fraction are by scholars whose specialized interest and technical jargon are often enough to scare off the average reader. Thus for the latter it is not easy to find something comprehensive and compact on this land and people.

It is with a view to contributing what little we can to fill this gap that we are presenting in this book our observations and studies during our five years' sojourn in Tibet. Special emphasis has been laid on its religious and political organizations, both features which so far have not been properly treated. And in view of the latest far-reaching developments which have drawn the world's attention to that quarter, we have endeavored to bring our narrative almost up to the very date of going to press.

Two charges, we believe, may be preferred against us. First, there is too much a preponderance on Lhasa and its people. Second, we have dwelt chiefly on the sunny side of the picture. Regarding the first charge, our excuse is that Lhasa, which we happen to know best, is the religious, cultural, and political center of contemporary Tibet. Our emphasis is quite commensurate with its importance. As to the second charge, we believe enough has already been said on the other side so our emphasis on the more cheerful aspects is warranted.

This book is not intended for specialists on Tibet. We therefore have endeavored to include only a minimum of Tibetan names in the text. We try to reproduce the approximate sounds by the simplest English spelling. No scientific transliteration is attempted.

We are grateful to Professor George E. Taylor, Director of Far Eastern Institute, University of Washington, for having kindly written an introduction. We want to acknowledge our indebtedness to Professor Ferdinand D. Lessing, Agassiz Professor of Oriental Languages, University of California, for his valuable suggestions regarding Tibetan religion. We wish also to express our thanks to Mr. P. Aufschnaiter for preparing two maps for us. With the help of these maps the outline map in this book has been made. Our heartfelt thanks are due a host of Tibetan friends who have rendered us assistance not only in collecting information but also in checking errors.

To Tibet, which has made an ineffaceable imprint on our soul with its majestic grandeur and sublime serenity, and its people, pious and hospitable, in whose midst we have spent the most memorable years of our life, we dedicate this book.

T. L. S. and S. C. L.

Santa Rosa, California
March 19, 1952

# Contents

**TIBET** AND THE TIBETANS

## part one

## *Unrolling the Tibetan Map*

### First Glimmers of Unknown Tibet

Tibet today remains shrouded in obscurity, perhaps as much in a geographical sense as in any other. A systematic survey has never been attempted. Only a few fortunate adventurers have been able to fight their way into the country against the obstacles of hostile authorities, a suspicious populace, and primitive Nature in all its ferocity. Those few caught glimpses of mighty rivers and gorges, mountains with eternal snow and glaciers, turquoise lakes, deserts, weird lamas and lamaseries, uncouth animals and men. Some of them died; others, after stirring adventures, brought back notes and sketches which enable some patient scholars to trace out a map of modern Tibet.

The earliest known allusion to Tibet in written records is from a Chinese source and concerns the banishment of the tribes of San Miao to San Wei by the Emperor Shun about 2255 B.C. Chinese historians and geographers identify San Wei with the Tibetan highland. Later Chinese chronicles refer to that region summarily as the land of the Kyang tribes.

The first Western geographer to mention this part of the world was Herodotus in the fifth century B.C. He told of a Hindu tradition that in the cloudland north of India there existed gold-digging ants smaller than dogs but bigger than foxes. These legendary ants have later been identified as marmots, burrowing animals that throw up heaps of earth which may contain some gold dust, or as human gold diggers crouching under cover of animal skins. Both the animals and the men are to be met within the northern plain of Tibet even today.

The first authentic record of Tibet and Tibetan geography is from the seventh century A.D. When the westward expansion of the Ta Tang* Empire (618–906) came into collision with the To Fan Empire, China first took note of a powerful neighbor with whom she was destined to entertain the closest relations. *To Fan* (or, according to a variant in the old pronunciation of the second word, *To Bo*) is the land's Chinese name most like the English word *Tibet*. A plausible explanation is that *To* is a phonetic rendering of a Tibetan word for highland, while *Bo* is the name the Tibetans give to themselves. In Sanskrit manuscripts of about the seventh century, Tibet is called *Bhota*. The English word *Tibet*, of Turkish origin, is a corruption of both syllables.

During the seventh and eighth centuries, many wars were fought and many peace missions exchanged between China and Tibet. Both the old and new compilations of *History of the Tang Dynasty* devote special chapters to the Tibetan people and contain sidelights on the geography of the country. It is here that the name and the location of the capital, Lhasa (Land of God), and those of the main river, Tsangpo, are recorded for the first time. A number of other place names of Tibet are mentioned, but unfortunately most are unidentifiable.

As we shall see in our chapter on history, the To Bo Empire, which made so glorious a beginning in the seventh century, did not flourish long. Barely two hundred years passed before it was all but forgotten by China and by the world. Tibet is not mentioned again until the *History of the Yuan Dynasty* (1206–1367), which enumerates the administrative divisions of Tibet made by the Mongol emperors. Again many of the geographic names are not identifiable. It was no doubt the Yuan chroniclers who first popularized the term *lama*, which the world has come to associate with Tibet. When the Mongols came to Tibet, they found it no longer a country of warriors but a land of lamas, or spiritual teachers.

In the year 1245, one Piano Carpini, sent by the Roman Pope to the Great Khan of the East, learned about the land of Tibet and a horrible custom practiced there. He reported that in that country "when anyone's father is about to give up the ghost, all the relatives meet together and they eat him, as was told to me for certain." During the years 1253–55, a Franciscan monk, William de Rubruquis, on his journey to see the Great Khan, learned that beyond the Tangut region to the northwest dwelt the Tibetans, a people in

* Ta Tang, meaning the Great Tang Empire, or China under the Tang Dynasty.

4                                                                        *Tibet and the Tibetans*

the habit of eating their dead parents and making handsome cups of their skulls in memory of them. He also heard that they had much gold in their country, and he even saw "many misshapen individuals of this people." Such reports do not seem to tally with Chinese records of the same period. Cannibals could hardly have made spiritual masters. We may dismiss these reports as exaggerations founded on certain practices in Lamaist occultism; or the people described may have been some backward tribes related to the Tibetans and living on the borders of Tibet.

The description of Tibet made by the greatest traveler of the Middle Ages, Marco Polo, who sojourned at the court of Kublai Khan from 1275 to 1295, contains much more reliable information. Though he called them "idolaters," "great thieves," and "an ill-conditioned race," he described the people of Tibet as having a language of their own and living in a great country embracing eight kingdoms and a vast number of cities and villages. He also said that among this people there existed the best enchanters and astrologers of the world, who could perform such marvels by their diabolic art that he did not deem it fit to narrate them in his book.

## Emperor K'ang Hsi Orders the First Tibetan Map

The Western writers whom we have named thus far wrote only from hearsay. In the year 1325, however, a Franciscan monk, Odorico de Pordenone, traveled from northwest China across Tibet to Europe, where he arrived in 1330. He called the country Riboth, an approximation of the old Tibetan pronunciation of the tribal name, and mentioned one Lhasa Gota. This first white man to see Tibet described the Tibetans as living in tents of black felt but having a very fine chief city called Gota, all of white stone, with well-paved streets, wherein none dared shed human blood. This gives some idea of Lhasa even today. Regarding the eating of dead parents, Odorico related that the priests cut off the head of the deceased and gave it to the son, who made a drinking cup of it. The body was cut up and thrown to eagles and vultures.

From the fourteenth century to the seventeenth, China under the Ming Dynasty (1368–1644) maintained a generally cordial relation with Tibet. The *History of Ming* records many peaceful missions to and from this land of the lamas. Though the routes can easily be traced, the place names are sometimes confusing.

The first Europeans to bring scientific information about Tibetan geography to the world were the two Jesuit missionaries, Johannes Grueber and

Albert Dorville (or D'Orville). Father Grueber was mathematical assistant at the Court of Peking when in 1661 he was recalled to Rome to receive instructions. The usual sea route being closed because of trouble between the Chinese and the Dutch, he was instructed to find a new route to Europe overland. The "new route" he found lay from Sining, now capital of Chinghai province, to Lhasa, a more westerly and less popular route than the one across the lacustrine sources of the Yellow River. From Lhasa he and his companion followed an old route to Nepal and thence to India. His astronomical calculations, made with an astrolabe, exhibit a general error of only about half a degree. This was no doubt the first time that a scientific instrument was employed in surveying any part of Tibet.

The earliest attempt to map the whole of Tibet scientifically was made by order of the far-seeing Chinese Emperor K'ang Hsi. Between 1708 and 1716 data were slowly collected, principally by two lamas educated in Peking, who surveyed the mountainous country from Sining to Lhasa and the sources of the Ganges. A map was completed in 1717, the first map of Tibet. Using this map, a copy of which was sent to the king of France, D'Anville prepared his famous atlas of 1733, which held the field until the second quarter of the nineteenth century.

From the beginning of the seventeenth century, the Catholic missionaries had been trying to penetrate this stronghold of paganism. Operating from India, the Jesuits and Capuchins made many attempts to establish missions in western and central Tibet. All the missions had to be abandoned one after another because of difficulty in maintenance or local opposition, the last being closed in 1745. But one Jesuit Father who deserved special mention here was Ippolito Desideri. He traveled from Kashmir right through western Tibet to Lhasa in 1716. Before his recall in 1721, he had become so proficient in the language and religious theories of the Tibetans that he often held disputations with Tibetan doctors of theology. A true pioneer of Western studies on Tibet, he wrote the first comprehensive report on the country. He has also the honor of being the first to try to identify the Tibetan river, Tsangpo, with the Brahmaputra instead of with the Irrawaddy.

Among the Capuchin missionaries, we should mention one Cassiano Beligatti, whose description of the route from Nepal to Lhasa remains true to this day. Despite the many travels the Capuchins made in Tibet, their contribution to its geography, as incorporated in Georgi's *Alphabetum Tibetanum*, is somewhat meager.

# Whence the Mightiest Rivers of Asia Flow

The publication of *Elements of Hydrography* by the Chinese scholar Chi Chao-nan in 1762 marks an advance in the study of Tibet as the most considerable water reservoir in the world. Nearly all the great rivers of Asia flow from Tibet. Fanning out from the Yellow River of China on the east to the sources of the Indus of India on the west, the Tibetan tableland contributes inexhaustibly to the mightiest streams of the East.

In the second half of the eighteenth century, the initiative in the exploration of Tibet gradually shifted to the West. Two missions were sent in 1774 and 1783 to open trade relations between India and Tibet. The first mission, headed by George Bogle, took the most used route between Tibet and India via the Dro-Mo valley, a part of Tibet that juts forth between the twin Himalayan states of Sikkim and Bhutan. The second mission under Samuel Turner followed the same route. Turner drew a map which was used one hundred twenty years later by Younghusband when he led the British expedition to Lhasa in 1904.

In 1792 a Chinese army under Prince Fu-kang-an marched from China to central Tibet to expel a Gurkha invasion. Much important information on the geography of Tibet gathered in this campaign was collected by an anonymous author in one of the best Chinese books on Tibet, *A General Treatise on U and Tsang*. U and Tsang are the Tibetan names of the two districts which compose what is generally known as central Tibet.

At about the middle of the nineteenth century, the Survey of India began to take an active interest in the region north of the Himalayas. Inspired by the example of the lama surveyors from Peking, they trained a host of native surveyors, mostly Indians and Sikkimese, and sent them across the Himalayan passes in disguise as traders, pilgrims, and lamas. Nain Sing, Krishna, Urgyen, Sarat Chandra Das, and Kinthup, to name a few, all distinguished themselves in their respective fields.

Nain Sing, who between 1865 and 1874 made several excursions from Nepal and Ladakh, was chiefly remembered for his exploration in the so-called lake region north of the Tsangpo. To him really belongs the credit of establishing the identity of the Tsangpo and the Brahmaputra beyond disputation. Krishna in 1878 mapped the first good plan of Lhasa. His reports on eastern Tibet, comprising the province of Sikang, are excellent. Urgyen in 1883 devoted himself to the region of central Tibet south of the Tsangpo; while Sarat Chandra Das, who made his way to Lhasa in 1881, turned out eventually to be one of the best scholars on Tibet. In 1880 Kinthup followed the Tsangpo from the famous southward bend at 95 degrees east longitude, and after four years of adventure succeeded in tracing it almost to the end of its lower course in the Assam plain.

The middle of the nineteenth century also witnessed the coming of many Europeans in an exploration race of this fabulous land, with the British and the Russians competing for the leading role.

The Russians took special interest in the northeastern region. Prejhevalski in 1879 became the first to enlighten the world on the orography of the northern fringe of Tibet. Between 1889 and 1894, several expeditions were led by Roborovski and Koslov to the steppes of the Koko Nor, to the sources of the Yellow River, and to the eastern edge of the Brahmaputra basin. Further explorations on the Koko Nor and the ranges south and north of this lake were made by Obrucheff and Koslov, respectively, in 1902 and 1909.

The American scholar Rockhill also twice entered Tibet from that direction. In his second journey, in 1892, he was stopped by the Tibetans on the Chinghai-Tibet border and returned eastward via Sikang province, thus exploring a region that was then very little known to the West. Rockhill remains one of the best authorities on Tibet. He was not only a geographer but also a scholar of the Chinese and Tibetan languages.

Many Englishmen used Ladakh on the extreme west as a springboard for exploring Tibet. Bower in 1891 and Wellby in 1896 marched from west to east across that vast desolate northern plain known as Chang Tang, and confirmed the prevailing orographical feature there as one of low folds running in a direction generally west to east. Still farther north is the area explored by Stein. Between 1906 and 1908, Stein made accurate surveys from western Sinkiang to Kansu province. His contribution to our knowledge of the Kuenlun range is, therefore, more thorough.

Somewhat similar to Stein's exploits in the Kuenlun was Sven Hedin's exploration of the Trans-Himalaya. From 1906 to 1908, Hedin made eight crossings at different points on this great divide between northern and southern Tibet and found it a connected system of different ranges.

Certain others made eastern Tibet their special study. Two Frenchmen, Dutreuil de Rhins and Fernand Grenard, explored the source of the river Dza-chu on th Chinghai-Tibet-Sikang border, becoming the first to identify it with the Mekong. Though De Rhins was killed in an ambush by the hostile natives, Grenard returned with the results of his and De Rhin's work, which included some excellent maps.

Though many Englishmen were interested in eastern Tibet, notably Teichman and Pereira, their main field of operation lay nearer India. When Younghusband marched to Lhasa in 1904, he had with him Ryder and Rawling, who made the first accurate survey in southern Tibet. They also surveyed the

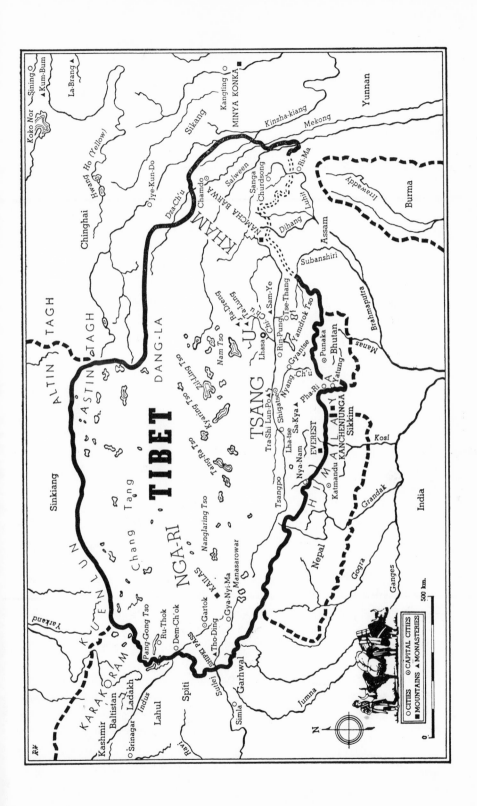

Tsangpo valley from Shigatse, Tibet's second largest city, upward, and from that part of western Tibet along the upper course of the Sutlej down to Simla.

All the vast area along the Tsangpo bend and its eastern affluents on the border of Assam seemed to the government of India to promise a short cut to the eastern route linking Tibet with Szechuan and Yunnan, as well as a territory of fertility and rich resources. Many were the assaults made in that direction.

As far back as the winter of 1885–86, Needham pushed far from northern Assam along an eastern affluent of the Brahmaputra to the meeting ground of Tibet, Burma, and India. Morshead in 1913 made a survey along the Tsangpo bend and incidentally spotted the eastern pillar of the Himalayas, Namcha Barwa. Kingdon Ward in 1924 covered the same region and then in 1933 penetrated farther east of Namcha Barwa. Other important travels were those of White between 1906 and 1908 along the Tibet-Bhutan border and that of Morshead in 1921 along the Tibetan borders north of Nepal and Sikkim.

## Three Boundaries of Tibet: Geographic, Ethnic, and Political

Geographically speaking, Tibet is a mass of mountains, all running from northwest to southeast, with deep or shallow valleys forming innumerable furrows between them. This mass of mountains is, in turn, ringed by some of the highest ranges in the world. A traveler coming from any direction invariably starts by climbing these outward ramparts—which vary greatly in depth and in height—till he gains a windy pass. The pass is often a water divide. Here he leaves behind the valleys and precipices, some of which are covered with vegetation, and looks ahead to a different topography of nearly horizontal expanses and low hills, all in a repulsive nudity. This is the Tibetan tableland.

Geologists tell us that this tableland was once the bottom of the Thetys sea. It is not quite as flat as a billiard table, and it loses its regularity, especially in the southeast, where by some freak of nature the meridional chains of Sikang province bar the way. The Himalaya chain sprawls along the entire southern frontier, a fit boundary for a country which bears the poetic name "Land of Snow." Toward the extreme west, the Ladakh range comes in a southeasterly direction from Baltistan. Karakoram, another mountain complex, lies north of the Ladakh range. Farther north the Kuenlun range, reputed one of the most ancient in the world, forms the northern flank of Tibet, as the Himalayas form the southern. The Kuenlun is composed of two ranges, the inner one being the Astin Tagh and the outer the Altin Tagh. The extreme eastern spur of Altin Tagh skirts Koko Nor (Blue Lake), the largest lake in geographic Tibet, and a good portion of Kansu province. To mark off the tableland on the east, geographers project a straight line from the Tsingling mountains in Kansu southward along the Min-kiang (Min river) to the towering peak of Minya Konka, south of Kangting, the capital of Sikang.

Coinciding somewhat with this geographic boundary but expanding its circumference much farther is the ethnic boundary of Tibet. All along the east the Tibetans stray far from their base west of the river Min-kiang to the Chengtu plain in the heart of Szechuan. Southward they cross the Himalayan barrier and constitute an important part of the populations of Bhutan, Sikkim, and Nepal. Along the Himalayas westward, they sprinkle the hill districts of Garhwal, Kulu, Spiti, Lahul, and Ladakh. Both geographically and ethnologically, the western boundary of Tibet should be the pass Zo-Gi-La, 11,580 feet high, which is considered the lowest of all Himalayan passes and is situated little more than thirty-five miles east of Srinagar, capital of Kashmir. All the valleys east of the Karakoram range and Baltistan are inhabited by Tibetans. Many mountains in this district bear Tibetan names. Lying toward the east of the Karakoram are large tracts of no man's land. Farther east is the immense Chang Tang (Northern Plain), where Tibetan and Mongol nomads mix. Pushing northeast along the Yellow River bend, they settle as far as the district Am-Do, flanked by those two important outposts of Lamaism, the Kum-Bum and La-Brang monasteries.

Politically, the effective control of the Lhasa administration extends over an area roughly one half of that described above. Starting clockwise from the northeast, its boundary runs well south of Jye-Kun-Do, an important trade center of Chinghai province. All regions to the northeast are part of Chinghai. Lying to the southeast of Jye-Kun-Do is the important Der-Ge principality astride the course of the Kinsha-kiang (River of Gold Sand), or upper Yangtze. By a local treaty signed in 1933, the north-south course of the river demarcates the province of Sikang to the east and Tibet to the west. Farther south, the border touches Yunnan and then bending westward extends to Ri-Ma. The region from Ri-Ma on the upper Luhit, an eastern affluent of the Brahmaputra, to the bend of the Tsangpo is inhabited by roving bands of primitive natives (Lo-Pa), occupying the hilly tracts east and west of the bend of the Tsangpo. Moving westward, the political boundary follows roughly the ridge of the Himalayas, with a few exceptions such as the Dro-Mo valley projecting south from the high tableland. On the Nepal border, trilingual landmarks in Chinese, Nepalese, and Tibetan are still to be seen. Farther west is Garhwal, the northern part of which is by tradition jointly administered by India and Tibet.

*Tibet and the Tibetans*

The frontier on the river Sutlej is the Shipki pass, 15,400 feet high, while that on the Indus is the village Dem-Ch'ok. Along the lake Panggong Tso the boundary lies west of Ru-Thok, the northernmost permanent settlement in western Tibet. Northward there lies a vast tract of uninhabitable land where the political frontier remains yet in a fluid state.

The Kuenlun range forms a natural boundary between Sinkiang and Tibet, except that eastward from 91 degrees longitude the Tibetan frontier recedes to a point just north of the Dang-la range. North of this range lies another wide tract of no man's land, which extends to the marshy lands southwest of Koko Nor. Only Mongolian nomads, who owe allegiance to Chinghai, are seen here, and these only occasionally. Then from the Dang-la the political boundary runs east-southeast to the Der-Ge principality. Lhasa extends its authority over the western portion of this principality, while the eastern portion forms a part of the Sikang province.


## U and Tsang—The Cradle of Tibetan Civilization

Historically Tibet was divided into thirteen administrative units, which were in turn grouped under the four main districts of U, Tsang (central Tibet), Kham (eastern Tibet), and Nga-Ri (western Tibet). The division of the four main districts remains largely the same today.

U, the district of which Lhasa is the capital, means "the center." Tsang, the district of which Shigatse is the capital, means "cleanliness," a name derived from that of the river Tsangpo, which traverses Tsang and U from west to east to form Tibet's economic artery.

The most important part of U is not, however, situated on the Tsangpo but on its northern affluent, the Chi-Ch'u* (Water of Pleasure). In the valley of the Chi-Ch'u is the cultural center of modern Tibet. On its upper course lies the monastery Ra-Dreng, which was founded in the eleventh century A.D. and is the fountainhead of an important lamaist sect called Ka-Dam-Pa. Toward the south, in the flourishing valley of Phon-Po, stands the Ta-Lung monastery, founded in 1178, once both a religious and a political stronghold. Into the east bend of the Chi-Ch'u flows the Dri-Kung, taking its name from the once powerful monastery Dri-Kung-Thee, founded in 1177, the center of an important branch of the Ka-Gyur-Pa sect. The Chi-Ch'u then meanders through the southern suburb of Lhasa, with the famous Three Seats of Learning: Gan-Dan monastery to the east, Se-Ra monastery to the north, and Dre-

* Or Kyichu.

Pung monastery to the west. The less famous but equally important twin academies of occultism, Gyu-To and Gyu-Me, stand within the city.

Just west of Lhasa, on the upper course of a south-flowing tributary to the Chi-Ch'u, is situated the monastery Tshu-Phu, seat of another powerful branch of the Ka-Gyur-Pa sect, which in the fifteenth century almost succeeded in unifying Tibet under its hegemony.

Three to four days' journey southeast of Lhasa stands the most ancient monastery of Tibet, Sam-Ye, first founded in the eighth century. About three days' journey northeast of Sam-Ye is the mysterious lake, Lha-Mo Nam Tso (Heavenly Lake of Goddess Pan-Dan Lha-Mo). This is not the only Tibetan lake bearing the name Heavenly Lake, nor is it the only one that is supposed to reveal the future, but it has assumed unparalleled importance for all Tibetans. When a new incarnation of Dalai Lama has to be found, the highest hierarchs of Tibet go there to read visions on the water to learn where to find him, and before each Dalai attains majority he also retires there to seek revelation of his future from his patron goddess, Pan-Dan Lha-Mo.

Opposite Sam-Ye, on the southern bank of the Tsangpo, is the flourishing commercial town of Tse-Thang. According to some, it has a larger population than Chamdo, the capital of Kham, thus superseding Chamdo as the third largest city in Tibet. Less than two miles away is the headquarters of the governor of the Southern Countries. Tse-Thang is situated at the mouth of the Yar-Lung Ch'u, a north-flowing tributary of the Tsangpo. The Yar-Lung basin is the cradle of ancient Tibetan civilization. Here the Tibetan kings maintained their courts long before the advent of Buddhism.

East of the Yar-Lung basin extends Dak-Po, a fairly rich agricultural region which adjoins the little-known Tsangpo bend. South of the bend is a holy mountain named Tsa-Ri. Every twelfth year, the Year of the Monkey, Tibetans organize a pilgrimage to the holy place, with government escort. For this is the fringe of the Himalaya hill districts where barbarous natives live who are forever jealous of their seclusion.

The Tsangpo, the longest river in Tibet, flows for eight hundred miles before entering India. Its many sources lie somewhere near the watershed of east-flowing and west-flowing streams on the western border of Tsang.

In its course through Tsang and U, the Tsangpo is swelled by many tributaries. Just as the Chi-Ch'u is the principal affluent from the north and forms the artery of U, so the Nyang-Ch'u (Water of Taste) is the principal affluent from the south and forms the artery of Tsang. Coming from the snowy mountains on the northern border of Bhutan, the river Nyang-Ch'u follows a northwesterly course through Gyantse, an economic and cultural center, and meets the Tsangpo just northeast of Shigatse, the capital of Tsang.

Since 1904 Gyantse, where U and Tsang join, has been the terminus of the Indo-Tibetan trade route. A route from Lhasa and another from Shigatse join here to link southward with the strategically important town of Pha-Ri, guarding the entrance to Tibet from the Dro-Mo valley as well as from Sikkim and Bhutan.

Shigatse is important, not only because it is the seat of a high political officer who supervises twelve administrative units in the district, but also because within a mile to the north is the self-contained religious-political center of Tra-Shi Lun-Po* (Mound of Blessing), the third largest monastery in Tibet proper. Here the Panchen Lama reigns as the religious head of Tsang (and, according to some, of all Tibet), forming the other pillar of Lamaism vis-à-vis the Dalai Lama at Lhasa. Like the Dalai, Panchen maintains a separate court with all its paraphernalia of clerical and lay functionaries.

Somewhat resembling Panchen and his court, but on a much more modest scale, is the Sa-Kya Lama in Tsang with his pitifully reduced kingdom. As the head of the Sa-Kya-Pa sect, his ancestors dominated all Tibet in the thirteenth century. His monastery Sa-Kya is still one of the most respected religious and cultural centers. It lies about three days' journey southwest of Shigatse.

Farther southwest lies the plain of Ding-Ri where several routes from Nepal converge. One of the routes through Nya-Nam (better known to the outside world by its Nepalese name of Kuti) is the ancient route taken by many great teachers of India who came to bring the blessed "Law" to the Land of Snow.

The Tsang district also includes a wide belt along the northern bank of the Tsangpo up to the Trans-Himalaya range. This belt borders on the valley where the Tshu-Phu monastery is situated on the east and the town of Lha-tse on the west. Lha-tse is important as the starting point for navigation on the upper section of the Tsangpo; from here one may travel by water as far as Shigatse. The lower section of the river where navigation is possible extends from the confluence of the Tsangpo and the Chi-Ch'u to a point near the Tsangpo bend. As we hardly need mention, navigation in Tibet is one-way traffic, that is, downstream only. Except in ferry service (where flat-bottomed wooden boats are occasionally used), coracles made of hides stretched on wooden frames are the most popular vessels. Such coracles, square and buoyant, often carry along with their cargo a goat whose duty it is to take the boat back to the starting point. There is a resemblance here to the leisurely caravans which require a string of cattle to carry fodder for those which transport the cargo. Small ferries cross the Tsangpo at many points as far upstream

* Also rendered as Teshu Lunpo.

as the western border of Tsang. At many such points, nomads from the Chang Tang plain ferry across to southern Tibet to barter their wool, salt, butter, and borax for tea, rice, and other staples.


## Kham and Nga-Ri—The Fertile East and the Desolate West

The immense tract of land 93–102 degrees east longitude and 29–32 degrees north latitude is known by the name of Kham. One special feature here is that the mountain ranges run from north to south, instead of from west to east.

The obstruction of these meridional chains and the deep ravines formed by the rivers Yangtze, Mekong, and Salween and their many tributaries have made this country difficult for the development of roads. The chief routes from China proper to central Tibet, therefore, keep well to the north where they cut through the head streams at much higher altitudes and thus with less ups and downs than would be the case lower down. But as the deep valleys have a more favorable climate, Kham is more populous than other parts of Tibet. Human habitation frequently keeps to slopes 8,000 to 9,000 feet above sea level, the bottoms of most of the valleys being too narrow for settlement. And owing to heavier rainfall, some portions of the district are covered with extensive forests.

The part of Kham which is under Lhasa's jurisdiction extends from the north-south course of the Kinsha-kiang on the east to the fertile regions called Kong-Po on the west, and from the environs of the district headquarters, Chamdo, on the north to the Tsangpo bend at Sanga Churdsong on the south. Chamdo, which is situated on the upper course of the Mekong, is generally considered the third important city of Tibet, ranking only after Lhasa and Shigatse. It is the seat of a governor of ministerial rank. Many important routes converge on this point: the northern and southern routes to Szechuan across Sikang, the route to Yunnan between the upper courses of the Mekong and the Salween, the route to Chinghai via Jye-Kun-Do, and the route to Lhasa through Kong-Po. The afore-mentioned southern route to Szechuan which passes through Batang (now Paan), by far the the most fertile and agriculturally developed oasis in all Tibet, is the most popular route between China proper and Tibet. In the eighteenth and nineteenth centuries, a regular corvée with resthouses and garrison posts was maintained the whole way from Kangting to Lhasa. A great volume of trade is still being carried on through this route today—silk and tea from China in exchange for the medicinal herbs, furs, and skins of Kong-Po and the incense of central Tibet.

East of the Kong-Po region is Po-Wo, subdivided into upper and lower portions. Tibetan authority seems to maintain a flimsy hold over this area, which is reported to be fabulously rich. A story persists that late in the eighteenth century about five hundred Chinese veterans lost their way in this unknown land and decided to make it their hermitage, but little information has since leaked out about this small band of world-weary recluses. Both Kong-Po and Po-Wo are irrigated by rivers that drain toward the Tsangpo bend.

Nga-Ri is the vast but sparsely populated highland in the west, bordering Ladakh and Kashmir. Its chief regions today consist of Ru-Thok at the lake Pang-Gong in the north, Pu-Rang at the south of the lake Manasarowar in the south, and Tho-Ding on the upper course of the Sutlej in the west.

The capital of Nga-Ri is Gartok, or, more simply, Gar. Only a lonely house stands there, the residence of the governor. Many tales remain to be told as to why Nga-Ri, which was the scene of the Tibetan Renaissance in the eleventh century, should have been reduced to such a position that its capital today bears the humiliating title of Gar (tent). The title of the district head is Gar-Pon (Governor of Tents). It is a very appropriate title too. Fairs are periodically held here, sometimes drawing two thousand people or more. Sturdy and uncouth northerners from Chang Tang with bare bronze chests and sinewy arms rub shoulders with Ladakhese, Kashmiri, Nepalese, and other hillmen of north India. Two of the most popular places for holding such fairs are Pu-Rang and Gya-Nyi-Ma, on the headwaters of the Sutlej. A government road links Nga-Ri with Tsang and U along the Tsangpo valley.

Both the rivers Indus and Sutlej rise in the heart of this highland. The Indus, from which India derives its name, has its principal source from the north of Mount Kailas, a snow-covered peak overlooking the lake Manasarowar on the south. The upper stream of the Sutlej with its short cut to India through the Shipki pass has its principal source well east of Manasarowar.

This lake, with its turquoise water mirroring the eternal snow of Mount Kailas, marks one of the most holy places in Tibet for pilgrimages. Both the lake and the peak are equally holy to Indians. In Hindu as well as in Buddhist cosmography, Mount Kailas is identified with Mount Sumeru, the cosmic center around which our world rotates. The lake is said to be formed by Brahma's soul, hence the name *Manasa-sarowara*. Both Indian and Tibetan legends have spun a halo over the spot, while poets and pilgrims pay glowing tributes to its unearthly beauty.

On the map of Tibet we see the words *Chang Tang* (Northern Plain) written in big letters across almost two-thirds of its whole surface. Travelers approaching Tibet through this wind-swept highland, the average altitude of which is 15,000 feet, see a re-enactment of the full drama of human civilization from its primitive nudity to a comparatively advanced stage of agriculture. First there is barrenness, then in turn come the hunter and the trapper living in caves, the nomads with their moving tents and cattle, the plowmen near their solitary settlements, and finally the modern man amidst a thriving community. Little civilization is possible in the wide tract between the Kuenlun and the Dang-la ranges. As a result of centuries of desiccation, the region swarms with innumerable dry lakes, like clusters of stars, forming a lake basin. This is only one of a series of such basins in Asia with no outlet to the sea, similar to those in Persia, Afghanistan, Sinkiang, and Mongolia. Their formation is obviously due to the lack of rain and the consequent drying up of the lakes. As most of these lakes were salt, saline crusts have formed on their shores, containing salt, borax, and soda, and these deposits form an important item in the commerce of the country. Some of the lakes are almost completely dried up and are known as salt pits.

The sources of the great rivers are on the outer slope of this lake basin. Besides the many rivers already referred to, the Yellow River (Sorrow of China) rises on the eastern fringe of the Dang-la range. South of the range human life begins, and its pulse quickens toward the Trans-Himalaya and the river Tsangpo. Some of the biggest lakes of Tibet are to be found in this region between the Dang-la and the Trans-Himalaya, notably Nam Tso (Heavenly Lake), which in size is only next to Koko Nor. Northeast of Nam Tso is Nag-Ch'u-Kha (Mouth of the Black Water), the seat of a governor who keeps guard over all approaches from the north to Lhasa.

Differing from the greater part of Tibet is the fertile valley of Dro-Mo which projects south over the Himalayan ridge. To enter Tibet by this gate is to know it by the most attractive façade—attractive but misleading. With a sudden abruptness near the ridge, the charming flower vales and forested hillsides give way to naked valleys and mountains typical of the Tibetan highland. Only the little-explored Tsangpo bend bears some resemblance to the Dro-Mo valley. Both are hunting grounds for florists and botanists.

Of the major factors determining the climate of Tibet, latitude and altitude compensate each other to some degree. If Tibet were shifted, say, fifteen degrees to the north, much of it, if not all, would be under ice; and if it were at sea level, it would be scorched by a summer heat like that of Egypt or Persia. As it is, the weather in the lower valleys of the Tsangpo basin as well as in eastern Tibet during the greater part of the year is surprisingly pleasant. Climate is generally rigorous, however, and changes radically in the north and northwest, which lie beyond the moderating influence of the Indian monsoon. Temperatures there sometimes reach —48 degrees F.; snowstorms may

*Tibet and the Tibetans*

last a full month; then for months there is not a drop of rain. The wind blows with gale force, and the sun scorches with an almost tropical intensity.

In this land of contrasts, the flora and fauna of many lands and climates are seen. There are numerous sheep and goats in Chang Tang. Wool heads the export list of Tibet. Yak, a hairy version of buffalo, is perhaps the second in quantity. The tail and hide of the yak also form important items in export. Equally numerous throughout the highland is the kyang, a cross between the ass and the horse. A wild animal of economic importance is the musk deer, which lives in the jungles of the Himalayas as well as in the barren uplands. Tibet is the chief producer of musk in the world today. Tibet is also a producer of furs, especially of stone marten, lynx, snow leopard, fox, and otter. Other common animals are the weasel, hare, antelope, gazelle, wolf, marmot, eagle, vulture, hawk, owl, barhead goose, yellow duck, chough, and common crow. The giant panda, a rare animal, is found in eastern Tibet.

The soil of Tibet is light brown or grayish, according to the humus content, which is invariably poor. It is alluvial soil, its parent material being sand blown by the wind over gravel and shingle. Barley is the most suitable crop for the whole country. Rice and wheat are grown in limited quantity at lower and warmer places; thus both have to be procured from Nepal, Sikkim, and Bhutan by barter for salt, borax, or wool from Chang Tang.

The mineral content of the land is relatively unexplored. Since many rivers from Tibet like the Yangtze and the Indus contain gold sands, it is reasonable to expect Tibet to be rich in gold. Iron, lead, and coal mines have been known to exist. And in places oil is also said to have been found. However, in the absence of any systematic prospecting, Tibet's mineral riches remain a subject for speculation.

# part two

## Reviewing Tibet's Past and Present

### Tibetan Genesis: The Monkey and the Mountain Ogress

The Tibetans, like men elsewhere, have their myths to explain the creation. One of these myths is the story of the cosmic egg. It is said that in the very beginning there was born from the void a most wonderful egg. After five months it burst open. Space, heat, fire, oceans, and mountains came from it; and from its very interior came a man.

This being, though a man, was also a snake or dragon. In some accounts it was a female snake or dragon, while in others it was a male. She or he was the first of human creatures and hence the ancestor of the Tibetan race.

Opposed to this theory of genesis, which savors of a pre-Buddhist, and possibly an indigenous, origin, is the story of the generation of the Tibetan people from a monkey and a mountain ogress. The story in its present form bears many marks of Buddhist sophistication. There was once a monkey who was a protégé of Avalokitesvara (Chen-Re-Zi, the Compassionate), the patron god of Tibet. This monkey was sent by his patron god to fulfill himself by meditation in the Land of Snow. There came a mountain ogress in the form of a beautiful woman to seduce him. But as no female charm could prevail against the sanctity of our monkey-recluse, she resorted to a woman's cunning. She threatened that because she was left with no alternative but to marry a demon, she would breed generation after generation of ogres and ogresses who would prey on every living creature in the Land of Snow. The monkey, succumbing to a compassion far greater than a mere desire for his own salvation, went to solicit his patron god's advice. The god commended him on his purity of motive and sent him back with his blessing. So it came to pass that the monkey married the mountain ogress, who bore him six children. In order to teach them how to be self-reliant, Father Monkey took his children to a forest of fruit trees and left them to live on fruit. A few years passed. When Father Monkey went to see how they were faring, he found to his great surprise that by the law of cause and effect his children and grandchildren had multiplied themselves to five hundred! Furthermore, they had eaten up all the fruit and were facing starvation. So Father Monkey once more hurried to his patron god and begged for succor. The god, taking pity on the misery of these victims of desire, plucked from Mount Sumeru five kinds of grains, which he caused to be sown in a field. The seeds took root and grew. The apes fed on them, and, wonderful to say, their tails as well as the hair on their bodies grew shorter and shorter. They began to speak, they made barley and wheat their daily food, and they covered their bodies with leaves. In short, they were men. Since they were the offspring of a saintly monkey and a voluptuous demoness, they inherited the virtues of fortitude, piety, charitableness, diligence, love for goodness, gentle speech, and eloquence from their father, and the vices of greediness, love for trade, lust, obstinacy, frivolousness, bad temper, and discourteousness from their mother. And with this, your Tibetan friend will explain the reason why the people of the hallowed land of Tibet are no better today than people elsewhere.

This story is said to have had its origin in Yar-Lung, and this was how the principal town there came to bear the name Tse-Thang. After Father Monkey had seen that the material needs of his children and grandchildren had been provided for, he taught them to play games there on the plain. What other interpretation can there be but that Tse-Thang is a combination of *Tse* (to play) and *Thang* (a plain)?

The history of a unified Tibet began in the same region under a prince allegedly coming from India. Accounts do not agree on the identity of this prince. He has been identified with Karna, son of Pandu, in Indian epic tradition; or King Rupati, who in the war between Kauravas and Pandavas fled to Tibet in disguise as a woman; or the son of King Prasenajit of Kosala; or a descendant of the Lacchavi branch of the Sakya family.

According to the story, this Indian prince was on one of the heights of the Himalayas when his eyes were attracted by the auspicious-looking plain of Yar-Lung, and he bent his steps toward it. As he was descending from the mountains, he was accosted by a band of herdsmen, no doubt descendants of the monkeys, who asked him where he came from. Being unable to speak their language he pointed vaguely toward the mountains over which he had come. The herdsmen, misunderstanding, hailed him as a prince from heaven. Improvising a wooden chair for him, they bore him back on their shoulders as their lord the king. Hence his name came to be Nya-Khri Tsan-Po (Neck-Throne Hero), a name we shall see most commonly adopted by noblemen and kings.

Thus we have a myth, a fable, and a legend which respectively account for the creation of the universe, the origin of the Tibetan people, and the coming of the first hero, the king.


## Fact vs. Fiction: Twenty-seven Legendary Kings and Five Mysterious Strangers

Scholars have been trying to disentangle the fact from the fiction in the preceding legends. Their conclusion is that the legends are a hodgepodge of the traditions of Bon-Po, the pre-Buddhist religion of Tibet, with Buddhist interpolation and, consequently, abundant traces of Indian and Chinese influences. We know that while Bon-Po is much akin to Taoism in China, Buddhism came to prevail in Tibet as a result of both Chinese and Indian infiltration.

All Tibetan chronicles with more or less uniformity list twenty-seven or more kings, following Nya-Khri Tsan-Po. Each list, though seldom complete, includes such names as Day, Night, Fish, Ass, Ram, and so forth, some of which recall Bon-Po cosmology. These names are arranged in five groupings, three of which bear unmistakable similarity to the Chinese scheme of naming their earliest emperors after the three groups, Heavenly, Earthly, and Human. This genealogy of Tibetan kings is generally regarded as a later elaboration of a lost tradition, or pure fabrication.

Chinese historians, usually much better informed about their neighbors than the latter are about themselves, are reticent about the Tibetans prior to the seventh century A.D. They knew only of a western tribe called Kyang, with which China had had rather close dealings from the first century A.D. There had certainly been no such thing as the united Tibet the Tangs came to know in the seventh century. The Old and New Chronicles of the Tang Dynasty (618–907), therefore, provide the first reliable information about the Tibetan people.

Both of these Chronicles record that the founder of the kingdom of Tibet was a certain Shi-Pu-Ye, reputed to have been born of heaven. These names have been reconstructed into a Tibetan form whose modern reading is *Pu-Gye*. This name is important because it occurs in some of the most ancient records in Tibet, concurrent with the Chronicles of the Tang Dynasty, and because it is found in a changed but recognizable form in the royal genealogy of Tibet referred to above. What is even more interesting is that *Pu-Gye* means the "Hairy King," an echo of the story of Father Monkey. Tibet long bore the nickname of *Pu-Gye-Bo* (Hairy King Tibet), and Tibetans were called *Dong-Mar* (the Red-Faced) by their neighbors, presumably from the custom of smearing their faces with red earth. But proverbially a monkey also has a red face. Could all this be coincidence? At any rate, Tibetan chronicles attribute to this Hairy King the discovery of the principal metals, the introduction of agriculture and irrigation, the building of the first capital of Tibet, and the spreading of the native faith, Bon-Po.

While records in Tibet from the seventh to ninth century name only Pu-Gye, later chronicles of the fourteenth and fifteenth centuries try to ignore him and put Nya-Khri Tsan-Po in his stead. A Dark Age, covering the whole span of the tenth century, splits Tibetan history in half. In the period before this Dark Age, Buddhism gradually made headway after a life-and-death struggle with Bon-Po; in the period after, not only did Buddhism oust or assimilate the native religion, but the Buddhist, or rather Lamaist, hierarchy replaced the feudal lords and chieftains as the rulers of Tibet. All Tibetan chronicles were compiled in the latter period. It had then become the fashion, in order to gain prestige, to trace everything to Sakya Muni, the Buddha, or the land of the Buddha. Tibetan chroniclers may understandably have built a royal genealogy for Tibet, to claim direct lineage from the Sakya family or its contemporaries. It is perhaps in the name *Pu-Gye*, which the Chronicles of the Tang Dynasty place near the end of the fourth century A.D., that we get the first glimmer about the remotest past of the Tibetan people.

Another king of the prehistoric era whose name all the Tibetan chronicles glorify is Lha-Tho-Tho-Ri-Nyen-Shey. He came in a period between Nya-Khri Tsan-Po—with the twenty-seven kings—and Son-Tsan Gam-Po, with whom Tibetan history proper begins. According to the legend that has made the name Lha-Tho-Tho-Ri-Nyen-Shey so important, one day while he was seated in his palace there fell from the sky in his presence a casket containing two books of Buddhist canon, an alms bowl, the six syllables of eternal truth (*Om Ma Ni Pa Me Hum*), a golden pagoda, and a clay image of Chintamani (the treasure). As no one knew the meaning of this god-gift, it was simply known as "the mysterious." A few years later, five strangers presented themselves before the king, volunteering to explain the meaning and the power of these objects. The king, although he paid both honor and reverence to the casket, did not seem to appreciate the mission of the strangers. They departed from the country as mysteriously as they had come. This legend seems to have been spun around some facts about the first appearance of Buddhism in Tibet. The strangers, who would be the earliest Buddhist missionaries to come to Tibet, are believed to have been either Nepalese or Chinese monks.

## Rise of the Tibetan Empire: Warrior Kings Invade China and India

Four more generations bring us to King Son-Tsan Gam-Po in the early part of the seventh century. Nam-Ri Son-Tsan, the father of Son-Tsan Gam-Po, is reputed to have reigned over Tibet for about fifty years, beginning in 570. Although facts about this reign are little known, Tibet must have been effectively unified and shaped into a strong power under his government. At the beginning of the seventh century, the Tibetan kingdom already stretched east to west from the borders of modern Yunnan and Szechuan to Kashmir and Persia, and north to south from the Tangut region on the south of Koko Nor to Nepal and the country of the Brahmans. The people were crude and given to war and plundering, and lived on the simplest food, which they ate with their hands. They smeared their faces with red earth; although they had built houses and cities, they preferred to live in tents. Each year the Tsan-Po (king) and his courtiers took a small oath when they sacrificed sheep, dogs, and monkeys, and every three years they took a great oath when they sacrificed horses, oxen, asses, and men. They had no system of writing, but for recording important facts they used notched pieces of wood and knotted cords. Having no calendar, they counted the beginning of each year from the time of harvest. Their religion was sorcery, and even high matters of policy were decided by their priests.

Against such a background Son-Tsan Gam-Po was born; he ascended the throne in about 620 and reigned until 650. Everything of account in Tibet is to be traced back to him; in fact, he marks the starting point of what we know as Tibet.

His reign was blessed with the two greatest statesmen Tibet has ever produced, Tho-Mi Sam-Bho-Ta and Gar-Don-Tsan. Tho-Mi Sam-Bho-Ta, together with sixteen companions, was sent to India by the king to study and work out an alphabet for the Tibetan language. He studied Indian characters and phonetics, and on his return he invented a Tibetan alphabet with four vowels and thirty consonants, based on the Brahmi characters then in use in Kashmir. He also wrote a comprehensive grammar. Although the greater part of the book was lost, two chapters remain and are the standard text for Tibetans even today. He himself was one of the most successful pioneers in the new writing, and translated some works from the large collection of Buddhist scriptures he brought back with him. The accomplished king, Son-Tsan Gam-Po, took such an active interest in this work that as soon as he became proficient in the writing, he too translated several Buddhist scriptures into Tibetan and wrote a few works of his own. One of these works is the famous code which is still considered the moral basis for both ecclesiastical and secular communities in Tibet.

Buddhism, then, must have made considerable inroads at the Tibetan court. Son-Tsan Gam-Po married a princess, Bhrikuti Devi, daughter of King Amsuvarman of Nepal and a devout Buddhist. She brought to Tibet several Buddhist images, the most important being that of Sakya Muni when eight years old. It is now enshrined in Ra-Mo-Ch'e, the second important temple in the city of Lhasa.

T'ai Tsung, the second and the most enterprising Chinese emperor of the Tang Dynasty, came to know Tibet after having sent a mission there in the eighth year of his reign, 633. The report about this little-known people must have been unfavorable, for when Son-Tsan Gam-Po, following the precedent of kings of the Turks and the Tukuhun (one of the Kyang tribes), asked for the hand of a Chinese princess, the request was declined. The Tibetan king thereupon bent his wrath first on the Tukuhun, whom he suspected of intriguing against him at the Chinese court, and then, after inflicting several defeats on the various Kyang tribes south of Koko Nor, he mustered a force of two hundred thousand to invade the northwest border of Szechuan. He won another battle against a local commander and was checked only when T'ai Tsung sent a strong reinforcement. After a year of stalemate, Son-Tsan Gam-Po sent another mission to the Chinese emperor renewing the request. T'ai Tsung, evidently much impressed by the military might of this rising neighbor and seeing how strong a following they had in the Kyang tribes, granted the request. The statesman Gar-Don-Tsan was the man whom the Tibetan king picked to head the mission. Both the Old and New Chronicles of the Tang Dynasty give a good impression of this remarkable Tibetan. A loyal and capable diplomat, he not only won for his lord a highly cultured Chinese princess but must also have played a dominant role in establishing a friendly relationship between Ta Tang and Tibet that lasted well after Son-Tsan Gam-Po's death in 650.

The bride was Princess Wen-Chen from a collateral branch of the Chinese imperial family. She was also a devout Buddhist. According to the Chronicles of the Tang Dynasty, she brought arts and crafts as well as her religion to Tibet. For her residence Son-Tsan Gam-Po built a palace with a walled city. This event is considered by some scholars to be the same as the removal of the Tibetan capital, recorded by Tibetan historians, from Yar-Lung to Lhasa and the building of the Potala palace on the Red Hill (Mar-Po-Ri). The same Chronicles also record that the king ordered his people to desist from the custom of painting their faces red and sent the children of his chiefs to be educated in China. Many learned monks came from China during this period to work on the translation of Buddhist books. To the average Tibetan today, the most important gift the Princess bore to Tibet was the image of Sakya Muni when he was twelve years old. This is now the central object of worship in Tsu-La-Khang, the central cathedral of Lhasa.

The statesman Gar-Don-Tsan and his son Ch'in-Ling acted as regents of Tibet for almost half a century. During the latter's regency, there was constant rivalry between China and Tibet for supremacy in Turkestan. In one of the many peace parleys he had with the delegates of Ta Tang, Ch'in-Ling made no bones about the motive of his policy. He reached the peak of his career in the year 670 when he successfully wrested from China the long-sought prize of the four garrisons of Kashgar, Khotan, Kucha, and Karashahr in Turkestan, thus amputating China's arm reaching westward. He lost the prize to China in 692, and seven years later lost his own life, driven to suicide by his king, who had grown suspicious of the regent's ambition.

Tibetan chronicles mention a Chinese invasion of Lhasa after the death of Son-Tsan Gam-Po; however, this invasion finds no support in Chinese history. At any rate, war seemed to be frequent between Ta Tang and the Tibetan empire until a royal alliance between another Tang princess, Chin-Chen, and Me-Ah-Tshom (reign, 704–55), Son-Tsan Gam-Po's great-great-grandson. The marriage took place in 710. We cannot understand why, in comparison with Wen-Chen, so little is remembered of Chin-Chen. One reason may be that during the reigns after Son-Tsan Gam-Po's the nobility which used to marry into the royal house began to occupy the political lime-light and so thrust royalty into the background. This tendency was further accentuated with the increasing hostility between the native religion, Bon-Po, and the imported religion, Buddhism. The nobility favored Bon-Po, while the royal house adhered to Buddhism. Tibetan chronicles record that Son-Tsan Gam-Po once ordered Bon-Po priests to stop plagiarizing Buddhist scripture, an order which occasioned much bloodshed; and when a pestilence broke out in the time of Me-Ah-Tshom, in 740–41 the nobility was so strong in accusing the new religion of bringing the calamity that all foreign Buddhist monks, and later even Tibetan monks, were banished.

Princess Chin-Chen gave birth to a king who turned out to be an even more devout Buddhist than she. The story of this mother and son, as told in Tibetan chronicles, can be read in an allegorical light, as the Tibetans themselves like to do with all historical events. The story goes that when Princess Chin-Chen was pregnant, another wife of Me-Ah-Tshom pretended to be with child also. Princess Chin-Chen ultimately gave birth to a son, whom the other wife seized by trickery and presented to the court as her own. The dispute grew until years later the king had to summon a special tribunal, before which the child owned Chin-Chen as his mother.

The child was Khri-Son De-Tsan (reign, 755–97), the second as well as the last great king of Tibet. His military campaigns carried the fame of Tibet much farther than had any accomplishments of his predecessors. These were the days when Chinese Emperor Ming Huang of the Tang Dynasty was serenading his beautiful consort, Yang Kuei-fei, and when China's strength was being sapped by rebellion. The Tibetan king, after contracting an alliance with the Arabs, who were also contending for supremacy in Central Asia, effectively cut off the western army of China right at its base, in modern Kansu province. In 763, his army occupied Chang An (Sian), the capital of Ta Tang Empire, for fifteen days, and even set up a puppet king before they were driven out. The struggle continued for almost forty years before Tibet was reduced to the defensive. At the height of his career, the king carried his campaign against Ta Tang west to Baltistan and Gilgit, after conquering western Tibet, and invaded the land south of the Himalayas to Bengal and Bihar in India. A stone pillar below the Potala stands as a monument to his military glory.

Lha-Tho-Tho-Ri-Nyen-Shey, Son-Tsan Gam-Po, and Khri-Son De-Tsan are fondly remembered by the Tibetans as the respective incarnations of Samantabhadra, Avalokitesvara, and Manjusri of the Buddhist pantheon. We have seen that the first two kings did much in introducing Buddhism, but it was the last who laid for it a real foundation. He invited a great theologian from India named Shantarakshita, and then upon the latter's recommendation summoned the great occultist, Padmasambhava. Tibetans call this occultist the "Precious Teacher" (Guru Rin-Po-Ch'e), and are unanimous in conceding him first place as the propagator of Buddhism in Tibet. He is the central figure of many myths, and his image and portrait are to be found wherever Lamaism is practiced, irrespective of sects or schisms.

The greatest act of this greatest figure of Lamaism was the building of the Sam-Ye monastery in 787 on the north bank of the Tsangpo, opposite Tse-

Thang. Tibetans tell many tall stories about how this great master chastized the native demons and demonesses in this Land of Snow who were hostile to the new faith and how he won them over to his side, stories which are acceptable to us only in an allegorical sense. During those days the reaction of Bon-Po was still very strong both in court and among the people. Khri-Son De-Tsan, on assumption of regal power, had to kill a few anti-Buddhist ministers before he could have his say about religion. Another important event, after the founding of Sam-Ye, was a debate held there between two schools of Buddhism, one represented by a Chinese Buddhist monk named Ta Chen and the other by an Indian scholar, Kamalashila. Ta Chen lost the debate and, as agreed on beforehand, quit the land with both his books and his followers. The Indian school has since prevailed. The king openly advocated the new religion and went so far as to give his own daughter to Padmasambhava for his religious consort. A little before that, Shantarakshita had initiated seven Tibetans into his order. This first ordination of the seven Sadmi, or disciples, much eulogized by Tibetan historians, seems to mark the real beginning of the spread of Buddhism in Tibet.

Khri-Son De-Tsan died in 797. For convenience this year may be considered the turning point in the brief history of the Tibetan empire.


## Decline of the Tibetan Empire:
## Assassination of the Most Wicked King by a Phantom Rider

Khri-Son De-Tsan was succeeded by his sons Mu-Ne Tsan-Po (reign, 797–804) and Se-Na-Le (804–17). A legend attached to the pious king Mu-Ne Tsan-Po says that during his reign he thrice equalized the rich and the poor of his people, and each time he found afterward that the rich were as rich and the poor as poor as before. Before he was allowed to carry his social experiments further, he was poisoned by his own mother.

The reign of Se-Na-Le was characterized by a continuation of the royal patronage of Buddhism. Se-Na-Le was survived by three sons. The eldest significantly renounced the throne in order to become a monk, thus leaving the claim to his younger brothers, Re-Pa-Gyen and Lang-Dar-Ma. Of these two we are not sure who was the elder. If we are to believe Tibetan sources, no two pretenders of more opposed characters could have been found for the Tibetan throne.

King Re-Pa-Gyen (reign, 817–36) proved to be another champion of Buddhism. It is difficult to explain why the Tibetan kings of that time favored

Buddhism and most of the nobility Bon-Po. A highly possible explanation is that the kings saw in the rising strength of the new religion a good opportunity to rid themselves of the aristocrats who were ever intriguing and counter-intriguing for more power. It was this king who raised the Buddhist rank and file to the status of a new aristocracy. He appointed a few Buddhists to important government posts to replace the nobles, and granted revenues to each monk from every seven families, an act which appears to be not totally unconnected with his uncle's social reforms. It was also during this reign that the translation of Buddhist terminology was standardized and works of former translators revised accordingly. As a consequence, many translations in the Tibetan Tripitaka (three collections of Buddhist Scriptures) date from this period. What is more, this pious king is known to posterity by the nickname "Long-Haired One," because it is said that in order to set an example for respecting the clergy, he wrapped his hair in long pieces of cloth on which he invited the holy men to sit.

Reaction came in 836 with a coup d'état led by the nobility. Re-Pa-Gyen was assassinated, and even the life of his recluse brother who had renounced the world was not spared. The conspirators then put their choice on the throne, Lang-Dar-Ma, the persecutor (reign, 836–42). Tibetan chroniclers were unanimous in painting him as the most wicked man ever born in this world. The Chronicles of the Tang Dynasty also described him as a man of cruel and lascivious nature and given to wine. He destroyed Buddhist temples, including Tsu-La-Khang and Ra-Mo-Ch'e in Lhasa, and ordered many monasteries to be closed and the monks to revert to the laity or face banishment. Persecution continued for several years, during which Buddhist leaders had to flee the country. The king appointed one of the murderers of his brothers as prime minister, and filled all important posts with anti-Buddhist noblemen. Tibetans condemn them summarily as incarnations of demons.

Then, according to Tibetan chronicles, a monk named Pei-Gyi Dor-Je had a vision while meditating in a cave about forty miles east of Lhasa. A goddess came to remind him that it was time to save the erring king from further sins. The next morning, emerging from his meditation, the monk made inquiries of his followers and learned all about the king's wickedness. He took deep pity on him. Using charcoal to blacken a white horse and soot to smear his face, he donned a black cape and a black cap, both with white lining. Thus attired, he hurried to Lhasa and saw Lang-Dar-Ma on one of his outdoor excursions. There he produced a concealed weapon from underneath his cape, shot one arrow into the king's bosom, and thus put an end to his wicked life. During the ensuing confusion the monk escaped. After swimming across a stream, which washed the black from his horse and from his face, and turning his cape and cap inside out, he made off for Kham, taking some of his holy books with him. A search for him was made in vain.

That happened in the year 842. The king left behind him a house divided and soon a kingdom divided. Our story here follows a familiar pattern. One of the queens of Lang-Dar-Ma was pregnant; and another queen feigned being with child also; the pretendress produced as her own son an infant, who, according to some, was her nephew and according to others the son of a vagabond. But she was powerful, and she ultimately had him crowned as king. Hence he came to be known to posterity as Yum-Ten (Supported by Mother). When the really pregnant queen gave birth to her son, she guarded him all night by lamplight against dangers to his life. The son grew up with the name Er-Sone (Protected by Light). Yum-Ten reigned under the regency of his mother and continued the anti-Buddhist policy with vigor. Er-Sone was pro-Buddhist and was soon acclaimed by his followers as the legitimate successor. Civil war ensued, powerful clans took sides in the issue, and petty kingdoms and dynasties sprang up from the splinters of the royal house.

Tibetan chroniclers have preserved for us no facts other than two strings of names descending from the quarreling brothers. Even the names are so different from those of their forefathers that they seem to bear no stamp of royalty.

The general trend of events seems to have been that while the Yum-Ten branch held sway in U and Tsang, the descendants of Er-Sone roamed far toward the west to establish a kingdom in Nga-Ri and Ladakh. But east or west, Buddhism was making headway toward every corner of Tibet and into every stratum of the Tibetan people, so that when fresh seeds were borne back to the field two hundred years later, the ground had been well prepared to yield a fine crop.

## Renaissance: Emergence of Religious Hierarchies After a Dark Age

Two trends must have been at work to account for the tremendous change that took place during the intermission from the middle of the ninth century to that of the eleventh. First, the fury of the struggle for power, started in the name of religion, had spent itself. Many powerful families must have been annihilated or have moved away from the court, which was then in fast dis-

*A lady oracle in ceremonial robes, before going into a trance. She gives guidance to the credulous Tibetan people in difficulties.*

*Je-Yab-Se-Sum (Holy Father and Sons Three)— Tson-Kha-Pa and his disciples Gye-Tshub and Khe-Dru.*

*Men of Tsang district*

A ferry on the Tsangpo, the longest river in Tibet.
It flows for 800 miles before crossing the Indian border.

*From picturesque*
*Ye-Pa monastery came*
*the monk who killed*
*Lang-Dar-Ma, the*
*persecutor of Buddhism.*

*Prayer time in the Central Cathedral*

*A Great Prayer hall en fête*

*A high incarnation lama of the Red Sect*

*The famous Ch'or-Ten at Gyantse, built in the fifteenth century. It is considered the most picturesque pagoda in all Tibet.*

*Young incarnation lama takes lessons from a learned tutor*

*Himalaya, the Abode of
Snow, extends along the
southern frontier of Tibet
for 1,500 miles like a
gigantic embracing arm.*

integration. Political strife thus overshadowed religious dispute and gave Buddhism a chance to go underground. Second, the Bon-Po followers during this period, resorting once more to their tactics of plagiarism, appropriated many Buddhist books, which they claimed to have dug out from places their ancient masters had hidden them. This removed many fundamental differences between the two religions and compromised the stand of Bon-Po.

Bon-Po, one form of Shamanism, is considered by some scholars to be a Tibetan copy of a later decadent phase of Chinese Taoism. It lacked depth, having, in default of a philosophic base, a mixture of exorcism and primitive worship. However, by borrowing too freely from the abundance of Buddhism, it was not long before Bon-Po lost its own characteristics and became absorbed into its rival. On the other hand, the Buddhist school represented by Padma-sambhava and his associates in the late eighth century bore many features akin to Bon-Po practice. Thus to a layman today it is impossible to tell where in an average Tibetan's religion Buddhism begins and Bon-Po ends. That is why we have been constrained to designate it by the special name of "Lamaism."

Little bitterness existed between these rival faiths when Buddhism staged its comeback after a lapse of two hundred years. European scholars have been wont to call this movement a Tibetan renaissance. And a renaissance it truly was. To Tibetans, who had no culture other than the Buddhist culture, this revival of Buddhism was a rebirth of their spiritual life in all its manifold aspects.

They therefore called this the "New Spread of Buddhism" as distinct from the "Old Spread" before the persecution of Lang-Dar-Ma. The Old School of Lamaism adhered to texts on Buddhist occultism, translated before the persecutor, while the New Schools adopted later revised translations. Tibetan history from this time on consists of little besides a record of the growth and fortunes of these different sects against a dimmed political background.

Revival of Buddhism started simultaneously in both the east and west. We have seen that the persecution of Lang-Dar-Ma in the ninth century forced many Buddhists to seek safety elsewhere. Teachers like the monk Pei-Gyi Dor-Je, who killed Lang-Dar-Ma, fled to Kham and started numerous communities in the east. From such a community emerged one important figure known as "La-Ch'en" (Great Teacher). Attracted by his fame, many students came from central Tibet and brought new life to Buddhism. This took place during the reign of the fifth generation after Yum-Ten, or roughly, in the last quarter of the tenth century. How powerful Buddhism had grown in the heart of Tibet, despite generations of persecution, may be deduced from the fact that some of these students were patronized by the very descendants of Yum-Ten, the anti-Buddhist king.

A much more successful movement came from the opposite direction, western Tibet. Starting from the fourth generation after Er-Sone, the kings of Gu-Ge (the kingdom founded by Er-Sone's descendants on the upper Sutlej in Nga-Ri) sent batches of young students to India, in general to rejuvenate Buddhism and in particular to clear up certain doubts on the teachings of the occultist school. One of the best of these returned students was Rin-Ch'en Zam-Po, whose translations of books on the Mystic School (Vajrayana), as well as those done by his associates and disciples, were adopted by all sects after Nying-Ma-Pa as standard texts.

The greatest event in this period took place in 1042 when the great Bengali teacher Atisha was invited to Gu-Ge by its king. Atisha, or, as the Tibetans more respectfully call him, "Jo-Wo-Je" (Venerable Master), is ranked in importance perhaps only second to Padmasambhava. An active missionary, Atisha carried his evangelic work far from the monastery Tho-Ding, then the cultural center of Gu-Ge, to central Tibet, including such places as Sam-Ye, Lhasa, and Nye-Thang. Nye-Thang, a village about half a day's journey southwest of Lhasa, is now hallowed by a pagoda containing the remains of the great teacher. His main contribution was a treatise on the various stages leading to final attainment, a work which inspired another important work by the great reformer, Tson-Kha-Pa, founder of the most prosperous sect in contemporary Tibet. Jo-Wo-Je and his main disciple, Drom-Ton, were the founders of the Ka-Dam-Pa sect.

We shall not be drawn into the maze of the numerous religious histories. Each sect is supposed to have preserved the essence of the Truth from a distinct line of masters. For our present purpose it suffices to know that there are four main sects of Lamaism: the Ka-Dam-Pa, the Sa-Kya-Pa, the Ka-Gyur-Pa, and the Ge-Lu-Pa. All of them play significant roles in Tibetan history.


The Patron and the Chaplain:
Political Unification Under Sa-Kya Papacy

In the year 1240 two Mongol generals, in one of their sallies in central Asia, marched into Tibet with their forces and routed a Tibetan army on the Chinghai-Tibetan border. The generals had long heard of this land of lamas, and they wanted to send back one of the greatest among them to their king,

Godan, nephew of Genghis Khan. The Lamaist community in Tibet was then represented by four dominant groups, each belonging to one sect or monastery. The Ka-Dam-Pa sect, which had its base at Ra-Dreng monastery, boasted of the largest following; the two monasteries of Ta-Lung and Dri-Kung-Thee, both belonging to the Ka-Gyur-Pa sect, were unequaled in prestige; but the most learned in law was the Pandit of the Sa-Kya monastery. Therefore, the Sa-Kya Pandit was summoned to Mongolia.

Exactly how Tibet passed into the hands of the religious hierarchies remains yet to be told. Anyway, in the middle of the thirteenth century, whatever power was still left in the hands of the lay chieftains was wedded to the cause of religion. And except for such unity as was extant in a religious sense, Tibet had ceased to exist as a unified country. Political unification of Tibet, under religious supremacy, was brought about by the Yuan emperors (1206–1367). The going of the Sa-Kya Pandit (Sa-Pan) was by no means the first surrender to Mongol supremacy. Overtures were made by individual Tibetan chieftains almost half a century earlier. It was the Sa-Kya Pandit, however, who, on behalf of all Tibet, gave definite shape to relations between the Mongol conquerors and Tibet.

Sa-Pan saw Godan, the king, in 1247 and as a vassal paid homage to him. On his return, he addressed a communication to all the spiritual and temporal lords of Tibet, wherein he admonished them to accept vassalage to the great Khan and hailed him as an incarnation of Bodhisattva and a great patron of Buddhism. If any hesitation existed on the part of Tibet, the matter was soon decided when Mongol troops followed Sa-Pan and completed an occupation.

Two years before the surrender of Sa-Pan, his nephew, Phas-Pa (Saint), had somehow preceded him to the Mongol court. Phas-Pa was not only a saint but a remarkable genius. While still in his teens, he so much impressed Kublai Khan, who was soon to become Emperor of China, that he was requested by the latter to initiate him into Lamaism and was thus acclaimed the Imperial Preceptor. He also won a debate before the Emperor over the Nestorians, Mohammedans, and the Taoist theologians of China. Emperor Kublai made Lamaism the national religion of his Empire and his Imperial Preceptor the Pope of all Buddhists under heaven. At the age of thirty-one, Phas-Pa was ordered to invent a writing system for the Mongols. He accomplished it within five years, basing it on the Tibetan alphabet. Honors were lavished on him, and at the same time he was made lord of all Tibet.

History has seldom recorded such a pair, patron and chaplain, in action. The Mongols embraced Lamaism with such whole-heartedness that within a century they had discarded all their martial characteristics. Besides their own conversion, they drove the whole of China along by making a spiritual-temporal alliance with Tibet which has lasted ever since. The Tibetans have come to rely in an increasing degree on the substantial aid and protection of the Chinese emperor. Although the emperor has changed many times and even ceased to exist, to the Tibetans the relationship, such as existed between patron and chaplain, remains.

Kublai ruled Tibet through the Ministry for the Spread of Government (Hsuan Chen Yuan). This Ministry, which governed the Buddhist religion and the administration of Tibet, was headed by the Imperial Preceptor. From him branched out a parallel system of lay and ecclesiastical officers. Directly responsible to the Ministry were four garrison officers, all laymen, two of whom were stationed at Nga-Ri and one each at U and Tsang. Next in rank was the Pon Ch'en of Sa-Kya monastery, who was local administrator for the Ministry. Under him were the ramifications of all the spiritual and temporal chiefs of Tibet. We wonder how much of the present unique politico-religious organization of Tibet was copied from Yuan administration.

The power of Yuan did not last long. With the decline of the Yuan Empire, the power of the Sa-Kya-Pa sect, with its base at the Sa-Kya monastery, also came to an end, in 1359. Even during its heyday the Sa-Kya-Pa had found growing rivalry from the two subsects of the Ka-Gyur-Pa—the Ka-Ma-Pa and the Dri-Kung-Pa. Emulating Sa-Kya's example of courting royal patronage, abbots of these two sects also paid direct homage to the Chinese emperor. The Dri-Kung-Pa sect grew so powerful by 1290 that Sa-Kya had to call Mongol troops to reduce it to submission, with much bloodshed.

Another threat to the declining Sa-Kya-Pa from 1349 on was the Pha-Mo-Dru-Pa family. Related to the Dri-Kung-Pa, the family had its base near Nye-Thang, and attained power under the leadership of Gyan-Ch'u Gye-Tshen, a most remarkable Tibetan. He first won a battle against the Sa-Kya, got himself appointed Tai-Si-Tu, an honorary title, by the Chinese emperor, and not long afterward, seizing the chance created by an internal revolt in the Sa-Kya monastery, marched in 1354 from his base in U, and in the name of pacifier, took control of all Tsang.

In the Chinese chronicles of the Yuan and Ming Dynasties, there are often complaints about the extent to which lama dignitaries, with their constant comings and goings and large retinues, were making themselves a public nuisance. The race for temporal power and wealth through royal patronage was continued by secular and religious chiefs throughout the whole of the thirteenth and the first half of the fourteenth centuries. Thanks to imperial favor, the lamas had come to constitute a privileged class, not only in Tibet but in all of China. Their dissoluteness and unholiness, added to their arrogance, made them such a scourge to the people of China that from time to time the court had to intervene. Under the Ming emperors (1368–1644), the Ka-Ma-Pa and Dri-Kung-Pa, the Sa-Kya-Pa, the Pha-Mo-Dru-Pa, and later the Ge-Lu-Pa all came to pay tribute. In some cases, the transport of several thousand people was involved, disrupting communication and causing considerable embarrassment to local administrations. In 1569, a royal decree had to be issued to reduce the tributes to once every three years, and to limit the number of retinues as well as the routes to be followed.

A great religious movement was gathering momentum in Tibet at this time. From the viewpoint of modern Tibet, no one can be more important in its history than Tson-Kha-Pa. Born in 1357 at Tson-Kha (Place of Onions) near Sining, he came to U and Tsang in his early teens; then after a mixed education in the Ka-Dam-Pa, Ka-Gyur-Pa, and Sa-Kya-Pa schools, he founded, in 1409, the Gan-Dan monastery, little more than a day's journey southeast of Lhasa. From this monastery radiated the light of a new sect known as the Ge-Lu-Pa (or Gan-Dan-Pae Lu, tradition of the Gan-Dan congregation), which produced many imposing personalities.

Two of the most renowned disciples of the great Reformer, Tson-Kha-Pa, were Gye-Tshub and Khe-Dru, both of whom were once his opponents. Nowadays images of this trinity (Je Yab-Se-Sum, Venerable Father and Sons—Three) are to be seen everywhere. Tibetans regard the relation between a spiritual master and his disciple the same as that between a father and son. Other outstanding members of the Ge-Lu-Pa sect were Jam-Yang Ch'or-Je, who in 1417 founded the monastery Dre-Pung west of Lhasa, and Gyam-Ch'en Ch'or-Je, who in 1418 founded Se-Ra north of Lhasa. Dre-Pung, Se-Ra, and Gan-Dan monasteries, named in order of their prosperity, are now regarded as the Three Seats of Learning (Sen-Dre-Ga Sum). In 1447 Gen-Tun Dru-Pa, Tson-Kha-Pa's youngest disciple, founded the Tra-Shi Lun-Po monastery at Shigatse. While Tra-Shi Lun-Po is now famous as the seat of the Panchen Lama, its founder is authoritatively recognized as the first incarnation of the Dalai Lama.

As early as 1409, in the seventh year of his reign, Chinese Emperor Chen Tsu of the Ming Dynasty had heard so much about Tson-Kha-Pa that he sent a special mission to invite him to China. In his stead, Tson-Kha-Pa sent his disciple, Gyam-Ch'en Ch'or-Je.

To resume our narrative of the Pha-Mo-Dru-Pa family, the power of this group declined toward the middle of the fifteenth century due to internal dissension, and passed into the hands of one of their ministers at Rin-Pung, in the region of Rong, between Gyantse and the river Tsangpo. In 1436, the Rin-Pung family seized Sam-Dru-Tse (now Shigatse) and gradually occupied the whole of Tsang. They were replaced in 1565 by their own minister, who had also started his conquest of Tsang from Sam-Dru-Tse and who became ancestor of the so-called Tsang-Pa kings. Both Rin-Pung-Pa and the Tsang-Pa kings were patrons of the Ka-Ma-Pa sect with its base at the Tshu-Phu monastery. Thus the reform sect, Ge-Lu-Pa, founded by Tson-Kha-Pa, had to wait until 1642 for fortune to turn in its favor.

## The Patron and the Chaplain Re-established: The Fifth Dalai Lama Made Priest-King

Starting from the thirteenth century, when the religious pontiffs of Tibet with the support of royal patronage came to assume unquestioned political power and replaced the royal house and feudal lords, the center of Tibetan politics gradually shifted toward interior China. We have seen how the Yuan emperors subjugated Tibet and put Sa-Kya patriarchs in power. The Ming emperors, though never exercising political control over Tibet, continued relations with the "chaplain." While conferring titles like "National Preceptor" (Kuo-Shih) and "Dean of Law" (Ch'or-Je) on the leaders of the Sa-Kya-Pa, Dri-Kung-Pa, Pha-Mo-Dru-Pa, and Ge-Lu-Pa alike, the Mings singled out the Ka-Ma-Pa sect for special favors. In 1406, Emperor Chen-Tsu proclaimed a Ka-Ma-Pa patriarch the "Great Precious Prince of Law" (Ta-Pao Fa-Wang), a title deemed higher than that conferred on the patriarch of the Sa-Kya. When the Manchus became rulers of China (1644–1911), they chose the Ge-Lu-Pa sect for royal patronage, and this, being the sect of the Dalai and the Panchen, is the prevailing sect today.

We must not be misled by this patron-chaplain relationship into thinking that the lamas have been the sole beneficiaries of the bargain. Many writers have already pointed out that, besides the Yuan emperors, the later dynasties of China patronized Lamaism with a political motive—to occupy the Tibetan people with their religious role and keep their martial qualities from reviving. Political considerations certainly weighed with China's policy in the days of both the Ming and the Ch'ing dynasties. How powerful Lamaism could be as a political weapon may be proved by the thoroughness with which it transformed Tibetans and Mongolians from fierce warriors into extreme pacifists. This particular brand of Buddhism seemed to have an amazing appeal for them and for the vast community of their kinsmen, which spanned the whole north and northwest front of China. So unless China was willing to renounce her north and northwest, whose control she had been fighting for since time immemorial, she could not but be realistic about a force which history had proved so vital to her interest. The emperors of the Ming and Ch'ing dynasties were equally outspoken about their motives in the pronouncements about their Tibetan policy. The patron-chaplain relationship, therefore, was never one way, but rather a reciprocal partnership.

The rise of the Ch'ing (Manchu) Dynasty was synchronized with the rise of the Ge-Lu-Pa sect, and the rise of the Ge-Lu-Pa sect meant largely the rise of the Dalai and Panchen institutions.

From the end of the fifteenth century to the middle of the seventeenth century, during the lifetime of the Second and the Third Dalai incarnations, the Ge-Lu-Pa sect led a precarious life, though silently gaining ground in Tibet, especially in U. The Pha-Mo-Dru family, comparatively friendly to the sect, was then tottering on its last legs, and the Tsang-Pa kings, who wielded authority between 1565 and 1642, extended patronage to the black-hatted and white-hatted Ka-Ma-Pa sect. From 1498 to 1518, the monks of Dre-Pung and Se-Ra, the two most flourishing monasteries of the Ge-Lu-Pa sect, were excluded from participating in the Grand Prayer at Lhasa on New Year days, an annual service said to have been started by Tson-Kha-Pa. Their position became worse from 1616 on, when the Tsang-Pa king extended his influence to the whole of the Chi-Ch'u valley.

Construction of the genealogy of the early Dalai incarnations has given rise to several different traditions. However, according to the official version of Lhasa, the first incarnation of the Dalai series was Gen-Tun Dru-Pa, who founded the Tra-Shi Lun-Po monastery; the second, Gen-Tun Gyam-Tsho, who often shuttled between the Tra-Shi Lun-Po and Dre-Pung monasteries; and the third, So-Nam Gyam-Tsho, who made Dre-Pung his permanent seat. Up to then the Dalai series was considered just one of many incarnation series in the community of Dre-Pung monastery. It was So-Nam Gyam-Tsho who first laid the foundation of the secular power of the Ge-Lu-Pa sect and the Dalai incarnation series such as we know today.

So-Nam Gyam-Tsho (Ocean of Fortune) twice went to Mongolia, in 1578 and 1587. On his first visit he saw the king of the Ordo Mongols, Altan, who had sent to Dre-Pung to invite him. The meeting took place at Koko Nor, and So-Nam Gyam-Tsho converted the king to the Ge-Lu-Pa sect. In return, So-Nam Gyam-Tsho was proclaimed *Vajradhara Dalai Lama* (Holder of the Thunder-Bolt, Ocean Lama) by the king. This was the first time that an incarnation of this series came to bear the name of *Dalai*, a Mongolian translation of *Gyam-Tsho* (the ocean), which was soon to gain popularity in China and throughout the world.

In 1587 Altan Khan (Prince Shun Yi), who was then doing obeisance to the Ming Dynasty (1368–1644), advised So-Nam Gyam-Tsho to request an audience with Emperor Sheng Tsung. So-Nam Gyam-Tsho received an invitation to the court, but while preparing to go in 1588, he died. Relations between the Dre-Pung monastery and the house of Altan Khan grew very intimate. The Fourth Dalai Lama came from the Altan family. This tie between the Mongols and the largest monastery of the Ge-Lu-Pa sect and the growing popularity of the Dalai Lama were certainly watched with misgivings by the Tsang-Pa kings. One of them resolved to ban the Dalai incarnations. Thus, according to one computation, fully three years intervened between the passing of the Fourth Dalai in 1614 and the birth of the Fifth Dalai in 1617, a circumstance which has no parallel in the whole history of Dalai successions. But one ranking lama of the Ge-Lu-Pa sect, named Lo-Zang Ch'or-Gyen, who enjoyed high favor with the king for having once cured him of a serious ailment, dissuaded him from persisting in his decision. In recognition of this great service to the cause of the Ge-Lu-Pa sect, Lo-Zang Ch'or-Gyen was later granted the diocese of Tra-Shi Lun-Po, some say by the Fifth Dalai; others, by the patron of the Fifth Dalai, Kushi Khan. Lo-Zang Ch'or-Gyen, according to the Lhasa version, was the First Panchen Lama, but the accepted version of Tra-Shi Lun-Po makes him the Fourth of the Panchen incarnations.

Nga-Wang Lo-Zang Gyam-Tsho, the Fifth Dalai Lama, is another epoch-marking figure in the history of Tibet. Just as ancient Tibet owed so much to King Son-Tsan Gam-Po, modern Tibet seems to owe all its present secular and ecclesiastical institutions to this "Great Fifth," as Tibetans call him. It was he and his regent, Sang-Gye Gyam-Tsho, who asked the aid of Kushi Khan, a Mongolian prince from Koko Nor, in defeating the Tsang-Pa kings. This was in 1641, during the reign of the last Ming emperor.

Quick to appraise the turning political tide in China, the Fifth Dalai Lama gave his allegiance to the rising Manchus. In 1642 and 1644 he sent greetings to the first two emperors of the Ch'ing Dynasty; and in 1652 he went personally to Peking, where he was proclaimed by an imperial order the Dalai Lama. A new patron-chaplain relationship was thus established. In 1713 Emperor K'ang Hsi extended his patronage to the other pillar of the Ge-Lu-Pa sect, Lo-Zang Ye-She, the Fifth Panchen and successor of Lo-Zang Ch'or-Gyen, proclaiming him Panchen Ratna (Great Pandit, the Gem).*

The succession of the Sixth Dalai in 1683, a youth who believed in women, wine, and song, occasioned serious dissension in Tibet. In 1705 La-Tsang

* *Panchen* is an abbreviation of *Pandit Ch'en Po* (Great Scholar), while *Ratna* is a Sanskrit word, rendered phonetically in Tibetan as *Erdeni*, an equivalent of *Rin Po Ch'en* meaning "the Gem." Tibetans called him *Panchen Rin-Po-Ch'e*.

Khan, a descendant of Kushi Khan, became so disgusted that he deposed the Sixth Dalai, and put on the papal throne a candidate of his own choice. The deposed Dalai died soon afterward in Chang Tang on his way to Peking, summoned by the Emperor. The interference of the Khan was resented by all the Ge-Lu-Pa, and representatives of the Three Seats of Learning and Tra-Shi Lun-Po went to the independent Junior Mongols of Ili in northwest Sinkiang for help. Although the king of the Junkars was related to La-Tsang Khan, he seized this opportunity for power. Crossing the vast uninhabited land of west Sinkiang and north Tibet in perfect secrecy, a Junkar army, composed of about six thousand men, swept down from the lake Nam Tso to Lhasa in 1716 and conquered Tibet. This was the first time the strength of the newly established politico-religious partnership between the Ch'ing Dynasty and the Ge-Lu-Pa sect was put to the test. Emperor K'ang Hsi sent a small relief army in 1717. His army was trapped by the Junkars near Nam Tso, and butchered to the last man. The emperor, now acting against his counselors' advice, sent a new army from Chinghai in 1718 and another from Szechuan. In 1720, having wiped out all the Junkars in Tibet, he put on the throne in the Potala palace at Lhasa a boy lama from Sikang, and proclaimed him the Seventh Dalai Lama. The dissolute young man who caused so much havoc in the lama country is still the recognized Sixth Dalai, while the one chosen by the La-Tsang Khan was later executed, as a scapegoat no doubt, and discounted.

The relationship between the generals of Kushi Khan, who now became master of Tibet, and the court around the Dalai Lama was never happy. In the background the Junkars continued their intrigues. Events took such a bad turn in 1726 that Emperor Yung Chen had to dispatch a minister to Tibet to arbitrate between the disputants. This dispatch of a civil, rather than a military, officer to keep a watch over the Tibetan administration marks the beginning of the appointment of an Amban (minister).

Friction continued between U and Tsang, and it gradually devolved on the powerful blocs of the twin pillars of Ge-Lu-Pa—the Dalai Lama and the Panchen Lama. When the Sixth Panchen journeyed to Peking in 1780 on the occasion of Emperor Chien Lung's seventieth birthday and was given a royal reception comparable to that accorded the Fifth Dalai by Emperor K'ang Hsi, there was real cause for anxiety over the position of the Dalai as unquestioned leader of the Ge-Lu-Pa sect. In the same year, however, the Panchen died of smallpox.

One brother of this Panchen was responsible for changing the fortune of the Tra-Shi Lun-Po monastery. Angered by his exclusion from what he considered a proper share in his deceased brother's rich endowments from the Chinese court, he conspired with the warlike Gurkhas south of the Himalayas and instigated a Nepalese invasion of Tsang in 1788. Provoked by Tibet's failure to comply with certain terms, the Gurkhas invaded once more in 1791 and this time sacked Tra-Shi Lun-Po, besides occupying the whole of western Tsang. The next year, Emperor Chien Lung sent his ablest generals, Fu-kang-an and Hai Lan-tsa, from Sining with an army of over ten thousand men. The army drove the Gurkhas over the Himalayas to the very neighborhood of Katmandu, the capital of Nepal, and returned after imposing some rather lenient terms.

Sweeping political reforms in Tibet were ordered by the emperor at the conclusion of the campaign. A country-wide census was taken; taxation was revised; Tibetan money was for the first time coined in Tibet; a local militia was organized; and Tibetans were no longer allowed to have direct relations with foreigners except through the resident Ambans. The Ambans were now not only raised to the same political status as that of the Dalai, but also, in cases of disputes over candidates for the Dalai and Panchen incarnations, to supervise the drawing of lots from a golden urn.

The Ge-Lu-Pa sect's ascendency in Tibet, which began with the defeat of the Tsang-Pa kings by Kushi Khan and culminated in the patron-chaplain relationship between the Dalai and Panchen on the one hand and the Chinese emperor on the other, was now complete. With their superb organization, the conquests of the Ge-Lu-Pa went much farther than U and Tsang, to Mongolia. In Kham and Nga-Ri, all the more important monasteries were incorporated into the Ge-Lu-Pa sect. On account of the flourishing careers of Dre-Pung, Se-Ra, and Gan-Dan, with their many affiliated institutions, the Dalai incarnation moved his court in Lhasa from Dre-Pung to the Potala, since the Dalai Lama rose to such prominence in the nineteenth century and after as to be representative not only of the Ge-Lu-Pa sect but also of the whole of Tibet, much as we know it today.

## The Hermit Caught in Giant Pincers: International Entanglement Since 1856

The patron-chaplain partnership lasted only as long as the patron was capable of being a patron and the chaplain willing to remain a chaplain. Trouble began with the decline of the Ch'ing Dynasty from the middle of the nineteenth century to the beginning of the twentieth.

In the nineteenth century, China under a corrupt and tottering regime lay prostrate against the onslaught of imperialist expansion. While the outer ramparts of her far-flung empire were battered down one after another, the Chinese mainland was being carved up into so-called "spheres of interest" by rival powers, the most outstanding of which were England and Russia. Forming giant pincers, closing steadily around China from north and south, the two jaws came to a clash at a point where the three empires meet—Tibet.

The first time China failed to give Tibet effective protection was in the year 1856 when Nepal, due to some trade disputes, imposed a treaty on Tibet whereby the Nepalese were entitled to extraterritorial rights in Tibet and an annual sum of 10,000 rupees. Since the treaty was signed under the paramountcy of the Chinese emperor, however, China's prestige remained more or less unimpaired; and, since Nepal was no less a hermit country than Tibet, the whole affair was considered of local importance only.

From the middle of the nineteenth century, as we have seen, the British and Russians took the lead in the exploration of Tibet. On the one hand, Czarist Russia, having established her dominance along the whole arc from Manchuria, Mongolia, and Sinkiang, wished to make a thrust to China's southwest through Tibet; on the other hand, England, who had peeled off a string of China's tributary states along the southern slopes of the Himalayas, from Burma to Ladakh, in the name of securing the defense of her Indian empire, also probed northward to China's little-known back yard. But as Russia was then heading straight into a war with Japan in Manchuria, England had all the initiative in the field.

By an annex to a treaty with China in 1876, England was granted the right to send an officer to Tibet on scientific exploration, but as such expeditions had become too frequent the Tibetans opposed it so energetically that China withdrew permission, though it was not without a price. In 1886 she signed a treaty recognizing England's annexation of Burma, which was her tributary state, a status somewhat similar to that of a protectorate.

The Tibetans were jubilant over their success in snubbing the British. But they had another score against the latter in regard to Sikkim. A tiny state on the southern slope of the Himalayas, sandwiched between Bhutan and Nepal, Sikkim was religiously, culturally, and ethnologically a part of Tibet, and a tributary to China. But due to its geographical proximity to India, it was being absorbed into the British orbit like Bhutan and Nepal, also tributaries to China. Whereas Bhutan, too, was religiously and ethnologically akin to Tibet and had always maintained a sort of self-government, Sikkim was looked on by the Tibetans as their dependency. In 1887 Tibet moved into Sikkim and tried to reassert her authority. England, after driving the Tibetans out of Sikkim in a miniature war in 1889, made China sign a treaty in 1890 which demarcated the boundary between Sikkim and Tibet and confirmed England's protectorate over Sikkim. The treaty was followed by a set of regulations in 1893, governing trade, communication, and pasturage. The highlights of the regulations were an undertaking by China to open a trade mart at Yatung in the Dro-Mo valley and the subjection of Tibetan pasturage in Sikkim to British authority. Now the Tibetans, who had been wont to pasture their cattle in the Sikkim valley long before the coming of the British in India, were outraged. They resorted to a sort of civil disobedience which paralyzed all trade. England protested, and China pleaded for time to bring around the Tibetans, but the latter persisted in obstruction. It was in the name of inducing the Tibetans to observe the terms of the treaties of 1890 and 1893 that the famous Younghusband's expedition was launched in 1904.

India had some trade interests with Tibet but certainly not enough to risk a war. Yet England visualized danger in the lurking figure of a Russian Buriat from Lake Baikal named Ngawang Dorjieff, who by virtue of his close relations with the Thirteenth Dalai Lama was carrying on much political flirtation between Lhasa and St. Petersburg. That was why England timed her action exactly with the outbreak of the Russo-Japanese War in Manchuria when both Chinese and Russian intervention in Tibet was out of the question.

The expedition of 1904, planned and executed by that enterprising group of empire builders in India in spite of strong home opposition, won some applause as a step in securing India's northern boundary. Starting in peaceful penetration, it ended in a triumphant march on Lhasa after sixteen engagements in which an unknown number of Tibetans were, as some foreign critics put it, "shot down like partridges." The Dalai Lama fled to China, leaving his representatives behind to sign the Lhasa Convention of 1904.

Two points in the Convention are of long-range importance. First, England established thereby a precedent of direct negotiation with Tibet over and above China. Second, England established the claim of the most favored nation with "special interests" in Tibet. By Article 9 of the Convention, Tibet agreed not to permit any foreign power to intervene in its affairs or to send out any representative or agents; to give any concessions for railways, roads, telegraphs, mining or other rights, to any foreign power without granting similar or equivalent concessions to England; to grant, without England's previous consent, any territorial and financial concessions to any foreign power. Besides, Tibet undertook the opening of two trade marts, at Gyantse and Gartok, in addition to that at Yatung, and the paying of a war indemnity of two and a half million rupees. This was the year in which Nepal and Bhutan passed silently from Chinese to British influence.

What had China been doing all this time? Harassed by foreign penetration and internal unrest, she was not in a position either to halt the British or to keep the Tibetans under control for negotiation. Imperial power in Tibet had declined considerably, the strength of the Chinese garrisons had petered out, and the resident Ambans were stranded at Lhasa. Thus, the British invaders, who had all along questioned China's sincerity in fulfilling the treaty obligations, were surprised to find the two Ambans in Lhasa little better than "a pair of honorable prisoners." The Lhasa Convention of 1904 made no pretense of respecting China's sovereign rights.

But now China was rudely awakened. England had weaned Ladakh, Burma, Sikkim, Bhutan, and Nepal, and now it seemed that Tibet was also going. Two years later, China contrived to sign with Britain the Peking Convention of 1906. The two higher authorities of London and Peking confirmed the Lhasa Convention, signed between the government of India and the Tibetan authority. And to China this meant Britain's admission of China's sovereign rights over Tibet. That was why she paid the war indemnity of two and a half million rupees; and that was why she signed with Britain the Tibet Trade Regulations of 1908, renewable every ten years, which allowed England to maintain armed guards and granted extraterritorial rights for the three trade agencies at Yatung, Gyantse, and Gartok; a telegraph-postal service; and a string of dak-bungalows from the Indian border up to Gyantse.

The treaties aroused considerable opposition in China because they had conceded further rights to England without getting anything in return. Resentment was also strong among a faction of the Indian Services, who insisted that China should be regarded as a foreign power to whom Article 9 of the Lhasa Convention would be applicable. But, however the views varied, the treaties remain the last to give shape and substance to Tibet's relations with England, and later with India, from the date of her independence down to the present day.

Having secured her hold on China, England scored another diplomatic victory elsewhere. In 1907, she signed with Russia, just after the latter's defeat by the Japanese, the St. Petersburg Convention, wherin all the "special interests" England had acquired in Tibet were recognized by Russia, while both committed themselves to keeping their hands off Tibet. A point of great interest in this Convention is that the word *suzerainty* was for the first time introduced to designate China's relation with Tibet, a word that has since been much bandied about without anybody's troubling to define it.

China was again belatedly aroused to action. She had been accused by the Tibetans of having failed to protect them from foreign invasion, and she had been accused by the British of having exercised no real authority in Tibet. So between 1906 and 1910, a capable governor, Chao Erh-feng, introduced sweeping reforms from Kangting, on the Szechuan border, to Gyam-Da, the headquarters of Kong-Po—a piece of territory which became later the province of Sikang. At the same time, a Szechuanese army of two thousand was sent to garrison Lhasa.

Now the Thirteenth Dalai Lama, who had returned after a long sojourn in Mongolia and Peking from 1904 to 1908, began to find his position untenable. He had lost imperial favor for having defined Peking's order in 1904 and had instigated obstructions to the reforms by Governor Chao in Kham, which cost the life of an Amban. In desperation he decided to seek sanctuary with his old foe, the British government of India. As soon as his flight to India was known, he was deposed in 1910 by the Chinese emperor, an act which killed his last hope of reconciliation.

The descent upon India of this illustrious exile blew much wind into the sails of those in the Indian Services clamoring for strong action. But England's hand had just been tied by the St. Petersburg Convention. Thus, after some exchange of notes with China, in which the latter insisted on regarding her action in Tibet as an internal issue, England veered to another point: she could no longer acquiesce in China's treating Nepal and Bhutan as her tributaries.

The next year (1911) the Chinese revolution broke out. When news of the emperor's abdication reached Lhasa, a mutiny started among the garrisons. Political strife soon deteriorated into personal vendetta. Left for months without pay and without a leader, the demoralized bands subjected Lhasa to a reign of terror. This situation continued for almost a year before the Tibetans, in alliance with certain disillusioned Chinese, took the situation in hand. The Thirteenth Dalai Lama returned in 1912, and issued a declaration of independence in which he listed as his chief grievance China's inability to protect Tibet from foreign aggression. All Chinese troops and officers were packed home via India. Then the Dalai Lama instituted what has often been called an anti-Chinese policy, and with what little justification we shall see below.

The Thirteenth Dalai, despite his seeming vacillation of policy, stands as an embodiment of the more enlightened vested interests of Tibet. China's weakness had been a disappointment. The excesses of the mutineers in 1911 had estranged many Tibetans, both secular and clerical. Ultimately, the emergence of a government in China at the head of which a Son of Heaven was replaced by a President, who could be any man of the street, was more than the average Tibetans could understand. Yet, when the first shock was over and passions subsided, there came the steadying force of millions of their kinsmen, from the border of Yunnan to Mongolia, with whom their fortunes have been closely interwoven. These "in-between" peoples, though politically and economically tied to China proper since the seventh century or even earlier, are, in race and religion, a part of Tibet. Neither Tibetans nor Chinese can afford to lose them. Chinese history has consistently proved that only when China and Tibet remain in amity can these peoples live in peace.

In 1913 the Chinese republican government restored the title of Dalai Lama to the Thirteenth Dalai. The military clique then in power in China was scheming for the restoration of monarchism under a new dynasty, and they were most anxious to buy British support. The British government saw another chance to enhance her position in Tibet. It pressed for a conference, which, after some delay, took place in Simla, India, during the winter of 1913. A treaty was drafted under British guidance, but the Chinese government refused to ratify it. The conference broke down first of all because *suzerainty* proved too restrictive an idea to force on Chinese public opinion, and then neither China nor Tibet could agree to the British plan of dividing Tibet into Inner and Outer Tibet, with the latter enjoying full autonomy. The first World War broke out in 1914, and the Tibetan dispute was relegated to the background.

Up to 1917, the Szechuanese army, on whom the responsibility of guarding Sikang now fell, had maintained garrisons as far as Gyam-Da, five days march east of Lahsa. Friction with Tibet was frequent in 1917–18, when the Tibetan troops drove triumphantly to the heart of Sikang, and in 1930–33, when they were thrown back to the west of the Kinsha-kiang (upper Yangtze). This has since remained the *de facto* boundary between Tibet and Sikang.

In spite of these local conflicts, Tibet's relations with China as a whole remained unaffected. In the meantime, all was not peaceful within Tibet itself. In the year 1924, the old rivalry between the provinces of U and Tsang, as personified by the Thirteenth Dalai Lama and the Ninth Panchen Lama, came to a showdown. As a result of this, the Panchen Lama fled with his court to China. There he lived as an exile till his death in 1937.

With the emergence of a more unified China, under the National Government, rapprochement became possible. In 1934, on the passing of the Thirteenth Dalai Lama, a mission was sent by the National government of China to convey condolences and restore official relations. An office was opened in Lhasa which later bore the designation of "Tibet Office of Commission on Mongolian and Tibetan Affairs." The Commission, which was of ministry status and composed of Chinese, Mongolian, and Tibetan members, had been organized previously to take charge of affairs relating to Mongolia and Tibet, both known as "Special Areas," as distinct from provincial units. England reacted quickly. Since she had initiated the idea of China's suzerainty, she by-passed it and demanded from Tibet the equal right of establishing a British Mission in Lhasa, presumably basing the claim on Article 9 of the Lhasa Convention of 1904. By the same action she implicitly relegated China's position to that of a foreign power, thus retrieving whatever ground she had lost in the Peking Convention of 1906. The establishment of a permanent British Mission in Lhasa was not mentioned even in the defunct draft treaty at Simla. The request held a certain charm for Lhasa. Here was an excuse to check fresh advances from the Chinese, on the grounds that for any concessions made to China, Tibet would have to grant equivalent ones to England. For instance, as the Chinese office at Lhasa had a radio station and a small dispensary, the British mission was also duly expanded; and scarcely had a Chinese officer of importance come to Lhasa than a British counterpart appeared.

In 1939 once more the important role of the "in-between races" was shown in formulating Sino-Tibetan relationship. The son of a Chinese-speaking family of the Am-Do tribe in Chinghai province was found by the regent Ra-Dreng to be the reincarnation of the Dalai Lama. A Chinese mission was sent from Nanking in 1940 to supervise the new Dalai's inauguration. A clear step forward seemed to have been made in the year 1947 when a delegation from Lhasa attended the Chinese National Assembly, participating in the drafting of a constitution and the election of a president. But before things could go far, the internal situation in China had come to such a pass that the question of Tibet faded once more into the background.

England meanwhile was finding her position in India untenable. On August 15, 1947, the date on which England transferred power to India, a quiet ceremony was observed in the few British outposts in Tibet. The Union Jack was taken down and the Indian tricolor hoisted; and the word British was replaced by the word Indian on the two permanent trade agencies at Yatung and Gyantse, on a temporary agency at Gartok and on the permanent mission at Lhasa. Thus India came to be represented there in what has been described by its own leaders as "undefined capacity."


## Aftermath of Revolution in China: Recent Political Developments

The rapid crumbling of the Nationalist government on the mainland from 1948 to 1949, ending in its flight to Formosa and the founding of the People's Republic of China under an authority of unprecedented unity and power, threw certain facts about Tibet into a new focus.

First was the problem of the return of the Panchen Lama. When the

*Two senior lamas*

*A Tibetan scholar spends much of his time in meditation.*

*The youthful Panchen Lama has returned to Tsang, his religious domain, there to resume relations with the Dalai Lama for maintaining the status, the functions, and the powers which existed between their predecessors "when they were in friendly and amicable relations with each other."*

*As prophesied by the Buddha, the Eternal Lord of all Buddhism, Holder of the Thunderbolt, Dalai Lama, the Great Fourteenth—a recent photograph.*

*The Dalai Lama's parents, brothers, and sisters*

*An autographed portrait,
with fingerprint, presented
to the author by His Holiness
the Dalai Lama at the age of
ten years.*

*Ceremonial dress of Tibetan officials*

*A high official making a social call*

*Tibetan army on parade*

*Young students learning calligraphy on rectangular slabs. Good handwriting is deemed a mark of scholarship.*

Portraits of Mao Tse-tung and Chu Teh
are paraded through the main thoroughfare
of Lhasa.

*Escorted by soldiers of Communist
China, the Panchen Lama arrived at
Lhasa on April 29, 1952. Banners
of the troops are displayed (left, below).
(Courtesy of Gyalo Thondup.)*

*The approach to Lhasa from the west. Lhasa, "the Land of God," has been the nerve center of Tibet for thirteen centuries.*

Ninth Panchen died in exile in 1937, he was on the Chinghai-Tibet border trying to get back to his diocese. But because of his long sojourn in China and Mongolia, where he won much prestige and support, the Lhasa authority naturally looked askance at him. A few years later three boys were successively found as candidates for his reincarnation, of whom one died an early death. Of the two remaining candidates, one, also from an Am-Do family in Chinghai province, was claimed by his court as the true reincarnation. During the last days of the Nationalist government on the mainland in 1949, he was officially installed at the Kum-Bum monastery in Chinghai as the Tenth Panchen Ngo-Erh-Teh-Ni or Ratna. A few months later when the Communist army approached Chinghai, he and his court went over to the new regime and openly advocated the liberation of Tibet. Lhasa meanwhile made a half-hearted attempt to put the rival candidate on the Tra-Shi Lun-Po throne. They were restrained by the consideration that this would mean a showdown with the powerful Lamaist communities in Sikang, Chinghai, and Mongolia, which backed the Tenth Panchen Lama at Kum-Bum, and would be a challenge to Peking. What is more, it would have further estranged the people in Tsang, who were looking forward to the return of the Panchen's old court.

In the second place there was the lingering effect of the Ra-Dreng episode. Ra-Dreng, under whose regency the present Dalai Lama was discovered, was suddenly arrested in 1947 for alleged conspiracy against his successor, Regent Ta-Dra. The ex-Regent was accused of being the leader of a strongly pro-Chinese faction. He soon died in prison at the Potala in Lhasa under mysterious circumstances. The episode led to a few days' bombardment of the Se-Ra monastery, one of the Three Seats of Learning, for supporting the ex-Regent, and to the storming of the latter's own monastery. Many from the monastery were captured and punished, but still more fled to China to join the Panchen's court. Nothing is more revealing about the political tension in Tibet than this splitting of the Dalai and the Panchen and that between the Regent and the ex-Regent.

In the third place, the unexpectedly swift liquidation of war-lordism in the northwest and southwest provinces of Ninghsia, Sinkiang, Chinghai, Szechuan, Sikang, and Yunnan exposed Tibet to the direct impact of a Chinese social-political revolution such as Tibet had never known in the past. No real authority had been exercised by any Chinese government over these border provinces since the fall of the Ch'ing (Manchu) Dynasty. Feudalistic and semi-independent, they had always served as Tibet's outer ramparts, to absorb, neutralize, or nullify all Chinese influences before they could reach Tibet. This time their influences as buffers melted away, one after the other, in less than half a year, leaving Tibet to face the unknown test alone.

Thus Lhasa was in a real dilemma. Since 1911 Lhasa has to all practical purposes enjoyed full independence. It has its own currency and customs; it runs its own telegraph and postal service; it maintains a civil service different from that of any other part of China; and it even keeps its own army. In policy Lhasa often acts even more independently. It has seen how China has been embroiled in continual war since the founding of the Republic in 1911 and how much her people have suffered. Lhasa believes that to be politically attached to China is more a liability than an asset.

When the rumblings of the Chinese revolution approached the border of Tibet, Lhasa, in July 1949, decided on the immediate explusion of all Nationalist officers from Tibet and made a public declaration of its neutrality. The voice of China from the Chinese mainland to Formosa, however, maintains that Tibet is a part of China. In early 1950 the Communist army reached the threshold of Tibet. It halted at the banks of Kinsha-kiang, just east of the Tibetan frontier fortress of Chamdo. There was some peace talk in the air. A Tibetan delegation went to India but nothing was settled. Then in the middle of October 1950 the Communist army advanced and marched into Chamdo, about 370 miles east of Lhasa, without a fight. Four thousand crack troops of Tibet were surrounded, and they surrendered with their commanders, while more than forty high-ranking officers, including a minister, were captured at the same time.

Lhasa had previously counted on several factors in its favor. First, there was the geographic barrier. The mountainous tracts to the east, the uninhabited highlands to the north, the rigorous climate, and the lack of provisions and means of communication were all formidable barriers. The warlords' private armies, the smuggling racketeers, and the many semi-independent tribes from the borders of Yunnan to Chinghai were sure to offer strong resistance. The rapid advance of the Communist army and the easy fall of Kham disproved all calculations.

Second, they had confidently counted on religious loyalty to the Dalai Lama of the people in China's west and northwest. In this they misjudged Peking's religious policy. There was no cry to suppress Buddhism. On the contrary, the Communist government issued several proclamations to safeguard religious freedom, to protect lama monasteries, and to respect the existing customs of Tibet. The prestige of the Dalai Lama as the pillar of Lamaist Buddhism was counteracted greatly by that of the Panchen Lama, the other pillar.

Third, it was Lhasa's hope that once a clash with Peking became a fact, some form of foreign assistance would be forthcoming. But since the British have pulled out of India, their interest in Tibet has become mainly academic.

Lhasa's hope naturally turned to India. Having inherited all the "special rights" in Tibet from England, India finds herself in a rather singular position. She knows those special rights to be the outcome of an imperialist policy. Being once a victim of the same policy and now advocating a crusade in Asia against such a policy, she can hardly enjoy the fruits of one without infringing her political conscience. The real concern of India is about Ladakh, Sikkim, and Bhutan, now all lying within the framework of the Republic of India but having close historic, religious, and ethnic ties with Tibet; and she has a long common boundary with south and southwest Tibet on which the last word is not yet said. She assumed those "special rights" in Tibet perhaps only with a view to future bargaining. Besides India, Nepal is the only country having direct relations with Tibet. Beset with serious internal problems of her own and having no vital stakes in Tibet, Nepal has neither the will nor the power to intervene. With no co-operation from India and Nepal, foreign assistance becomes an extremely remote possibility.

Thus, in every attempt those who upheld the status quo in Lhasa have lost ground to their opposition. In the last months of 1950, Regent Ta-Dra resigned to give place to the Fourteenth Dalai Lama, and the Lhasa government moved south to Dro-Mo. The first official act of the sixteen-year-old Dalai after coming to power was to grant a general amnesty to all political prisoners in Tibet. At the same time he appointed the minister captured at Chamdo to head a mission to Peking, to be followed by another mission under his commander in chief.

On May 23, 1951, a seventeen-point agreement was signed between the Central People's government of China and the Tibetan Regional government at Peking. The highlights may be summarized under four points. First, Tibet is to retain her autonomy, with no change in the Dalai Lama's political system or in his status, function, and power. Its religion, monastic institutions, and customs will be respected. Second, the old position of the Panchen Lama that was enjoyed in the friendly times between the Thirteenth Dalai Lama and the Ninth Panchen Lama is to be restored. Third, the Central People's government is to set up a military and administrative committee, with regional military headquarters in Tibet. The Tibetan army will be reorganized step by step into the People's Liberation Army. Fourth, Tibet's external relations are to be handled by the Central People's government. While all "imperialist aggressive forces" in Tibet must be eliminated, its commercial and trading relations with neighboring countries shall be regularized "on the basis of equality, mutual benefit, and mutual respect for territory and sovereignty."

From July 1951 events took a swift pace. The Dalai Lama returned with his whole court to Lhasa. Simultaneously three forces of the People's Liberation Army entered Tibet, one from Chamdo on the east, another from Ching-hai on the north, and still another from Nga-Ri on the west, to take over important garrisons in Tibet; while a fourth party comprising administrative and technical staffs arrived via India. Since that time control of the frontier along Nepal and India, formerly nonexistent, has been established; construction of motor roads and airfields is reported; plans about reforestation, mining, and improvement of irrigation and cattle raising are also said to be afoot; and some kind of land and educational reform may be inevitable in the near future. To all this, the long-heralded return of the Panchen Lama and his court will add new impetus.

The implementing of the above agreement marks the end of an era for Tibet and the beginning of a new one. It also enables us to predict something about Tibet in the years to come.

It must be realized now that there has been too great a tendency on the part of the outside world to equate Lhasa with Tibet. Though Lhasa, with its small population of twenty thousand, is admittedly the political, religious, cultural, and economic center of Tibet, it constitutes a small fraction of the whole Tibetan population, estimated variously between two and four million. The men who have been running the Lhasa government are drawn from the top class of less than a hundred still flourishing noble families and an ecclesiastical hierarchy of equal size. To them the Tibetan masses are the "hewers of wood and drawers of water." Cut off completely from world trends and from all the dormant social forces in Tibet, and basking in the waning sunshine of a theocratic-feudalistic autocracy, this privileged class can exist only on the ignorance and political lethargy of the Tibetan masses. Their privileged status is bound to collapse in this fast-changing world, and the process is going to be merely accelerated. However, social revolution is a thing that must grow from below; it cannot be totally imposed from above. It is not likely, therefore, that any radical change will come about in the Tibetan social make-up till something like a political consciousness is aroused among the Tibetan people. In an economically backward and highly decentralized region like Tibet, that may take many years. The feudal lords, who constitute an important section of the intelligentsia, may yet have a vital role to play even in this process.

What will happen to the clergy, who are celibate and drawn mostly from among the lower strata of Tibetan society, and the various strata of their monastic organizations? They have all along been held up as the strongest bulwark of conservatism in Tibet. But we should not lose sight of the fact that the clergy has always been more enterprising than the aristocracy. They could be most conservative as well as ultraradical; they are conservative when conservatism pays. Once the new social forces are unleashed, they are likely to break rank with the aristocrats, with whom there has always been keen rivalry. Already there is the rumor of Buddho-Marxism in the making. Such a movement will surely draw many ardent supporters from the younger and poorer clergy. And we shall not be surprised if serious dissension should break out in the near future among the conservative and radical elements, dissension which might spell the eventual dissolution of the time-honored monastic organization in Tibet.

There will also be some adjustments in Tibet's foreign relations. Trade and religious relations with Ladakh, Sikkim, and Bhutan will probably be left unaffected. But with India and Nepal, while existing commercial and religious relations may remain, all the unequal treaty rights of India, based on the Lhasa Convention of 1904 and the trade regulations of 1908, and those of Nepal, based on the treaty of 1856, will have to be revised in the context of the new developments. The undemarcated boundary between Tibet and India also demands a settlement. Thus, with the modification of economic and social patterns internally and the reorientation of external relations, although it is the avowed object of the Communist government of China to preserve Tibet's full autonomy, it seems unlikely that the Tibetans will remain for long the hermit nation desired by so many of their well-wishers. As to the exact role the new trend of events is drawing them to play, time will soon reveal.

# part three

## Lamas, Lamaism, and Lamaseries

### The Buddhist Outlook on Life and Salvation

Knowing something about the geographic and historical background of Tibet, we approach modern Tibet and Tibetans best through their religion. In Tibet, everything begins and ends with religion. Though in between we find much that is not religion, yet we can hardly imagine what would be left of modern Tibet and Tibetans if they were deprived of their lamas, lamaseries, and Lamaism.

Lamaism is a Tibetan version of Buddhism. Lamaism is Buddhism encumbered with the old faith of Tibet, Bon-Po; yet, in many competent opinions, a purer form of Buddhism may still be found in Tibet than anywhere else today. Thus some knowledge of the Buddhist outlook on life and deliverance may help us to understand the Tibetans' mind, their customs and traditions, their social, cultural, and political institutions.

To Buddhists, and of course to Tibetans, Buddhism is not merely another of the world's many religions which seek to save mankind. Mankind is too limited a concept for Buddhists, who think in terms of a much vaster kingdom of animate beings, stretching, so to speak, from an amoeba to Buddha. All beings within this domain are in possession of a mind, or soul. Buddhism is the law of salvation for each of these mind-possessors. The law is simply there: it can neither be made nor unmade even by Buddha. Only he knows it.

In the Buddhist cosmos, there are different forms of existence (Dhatu), in one of which each mind-possessor finds a place, as determined by his own merits or demerits. The lowest form is Hell, where one reaches the extreme of suffering; the highest is the realm of Buddha, where one attains the extreme of bliss. Starting from Hell upward are six forms of existence which lie within the current (Gati) of transmigration. We human beings are in the fourth form from the bottom. The three forms of existence below us comprise the realm of suffering, while the three higher forms comprise the realm of joy. Both the terms "suffering" and "joy," here, are to be understood only in a relative sense, for there can be nothing but varying degrees of misery for us transmigrants, as all beings in the current of transmigration may thus be called. Transmigration, in Buddhist parlance, means the change of abode of a mind from one tabernacle to another, as based on the total merits and demerits earned by the mind in all its previous transmigrations. Whenever the tabernacle has outgrown its usefulness and reached the stage commonly called death, the mind leaves it and enters into another tabernacle, an act which is commonly called birth.

In order to be delivered from the misery of being born and reborn in this current of transmigration, one must, by accumulation of appropriate merits, be raised above the sixth form and, hence, beyond the current. This is to attain Nirvana.

Many have already attained Nirvana. According to a prevalent classification, there are those who have attained Nirvana for themselves only, and others who, besides having attained Nirvana for themselves, wish to help every other mind-possessor in the current of transmigration to attain it. The latter are the Buddhas. There have already been several Buddhas in the past, and more will come in the future. Sakya Muni is the Buddha for the current span of eternity—the span to which we belong. He reveals to us the Law. Every mind-possessor has the inherent potentiality to attain Buddhahood; and we human beings might well congratulate ourselves for being already halfway up the scale. We should, therefore, strive to make the most of the opportunity for salvation, according to the way the Buddha has shown us. If our aim be to save our individual selves, there is the way of Hinayana (the Little Vehicle). But if we wish to save not only ourselves but also every mind-possessor in the current of transmigration, then there is the way of Mahayana (the Great Vehicle). Mahayana is just one stage above Hinayana. It is up to everyone to choose his own aim.

The most basic law the Buddha teaches is the law of cause and effect. According to the Christian equivalent of this law, "Whatsoever a man soweth, that shall he also reap." But Buddhism does not stop at that. It goes on to tell us that every being or every form of mental and physical activity represents the total effect of countless causes in the past, and is itself the cause of an unlimited number of future effects. Every cause *is* an effect and every effect a cause, in an endless chain.

All trouble arises from our folly. It is our folly that gives birth to our avarice, hate, and ignorance, the three propelling forces that cause us to go on and on in the current of transmigration. In order to remove our folly, Buddhism expounds the three truths of nonpermanency (Anityata), nonexistence of ego (Anatmata), and the perfect peace (Santi) of Nirvana.

A Buddhist looks on everything in the cosmos—both physical beings and actions—as in a state of perpetual flux, hurrying through ceaseless and countless changes, which may be summarized as birth and death or beginning and end. Neither a man nor an amoeba, a house, a government, a social movement, a sea, nor a mountain can escape this process. Now to be permanent, according to Buddhist definition, is to be both perpetual and unchangeable, without beginning or end. Since nothing is like that, everything is impermanent.

Then, to say that a given thing exists is to affirm that the thing has an ego (Atman), that is to say, a thing possessing certain distinct and unchangeable attributes and capable of coming into being by itself without relying on other factors. Evidently such a thing is nonexistent. Everything is constituted of something else; hence there is no ego. What we take for the ego of a thing is but a void into which extraneous factors stream to make something.

It is the aim of Buddhism to deliver all mind-possessors, including mankind, from the misery of transmigrations by showing us that nothing is permanent, and nothing really exists as such. Only when we have come to see this shall we have plucked out avarice, hatred, and ignorance, the propelling forces that drive us on in eternal transmigrations, and only then shall we attain the perfect peace and bliss of Nirvana.

Buddha and his disciples have laid down a full course of the science for gaining Nirvana. For the Mahayanists, however, two choices are open. One is Sutra, the exoteric course, which is shared by the Hinayanists; and the other Tantra, the esoteric course, which is reserved for "the proper vessels of law" among the Mahayanists. Both courses are contained in the Tripitaka. These three collections of Buddhist Scripture are, first, Buddha's own utterances revealing the truth; second, Buddhist disciplinary rules laid down by Buddha and his disciples; and third, commentaries and expositions on both by his important followers. In Tibet, the Tripitaka is classified into only two collections, the words of Buddha (Kan-Gyur) and the commentaries of others (Ten-Gyur).

As Tibetans are Mahayanists, they seem to show more enthusiasm for the esoteric than for the exoteric course. Regarding the relative merits of the two courses, one tradition relates that a practical-minded disciple of Buddha once asked him how long it would take to attain Buddhahood through the exoteric course and how long through the esoteric. The reply was for the exoteric a figure for which we can yet find no approximate expression; it is said to be the fifty-ninth power of 10. He said that by the esoteric course, however, one could achieve Buddhahood in one lifetime.

Hundreds of schools have arisen since the voice of the Enlightened One was extinguished. All of them try to give different interpretations to his words, but none professes to depart from the basic tenets which we have been rash enough to attempt to sketch.

## Ge-Lu-Pa, the Yellow Hat Sect

All sects in Tibet boast of being heir to a distinct tradition that can be traced back to Sakya Muni. But the heads of the prevailing sect, Ge-Lu-Pa, make a much bolder claim. The Panchen Lama and the Dalai Lama claim to be the incarnations, respectively, of Er-Pa-Me (Amithaba, Buddha of the Boundless Light) and Chen-Re-Zi (Bodhisattva Avalokitesvara, commonly known as the Compassionate). According to a Buddhist tradition, the Compassionate, a disciple of the Buddha of the Boundless Light, once made a vow before the latter to go back to the current of transmigrations to deliver all mind-possessors. Tibetan myths made the Compassionate the patron god of Tibet, the blessed land, and identified the Dalai Lama as the god's incarnation.

The Ge-Lu-Pa, of which the Dalai Lama is the *de facto* leader, is more commonly known as the Yellow Hat Sect. This name comes from the fact that Tson-Kha-Pa, the sect's founder, adopted the yellow hat for himself and his disciples as a mark of distinction from other sects that had degenerated through their preoccupation with mundane affairs. In this connection there is a story that the founder, failing to dye his hat any color to his liking, suddenly recalled that the great tenth-century master, Gon-Pa Rab-Se, who was noted above all for his chaste life, once wore a yellow hat. Tson-Kha-Pa then dyed his hat yellow. Designating the different religious sects in Tibet after the color of their hats, though it is often done, is sometimes misleading. Tibetans prefer to call all sects by their proper names.

Tson-Kha-Pa's reform was primarily directed against the rapid degeneration of the Lamaist priesthood from the thirteenth century. By personal example he restored disciplinary rules, laying special stress on celibacy and abstention from intoxicants and worldly and unreligious pursuits. Tibetan Buddhism being Mahayanic, there was then a sophistic tendency to look on all disciplinary rules as petty restrictions meant only for the Hinayanic followers. It was argued that for the Mahayanists, who are after the salvation of all mind-possessors from the current of transmigration, a much wider latitude of "expediency" should be allowed. How far the standard of this reformer is kept up today is open to question, but the Ge-Lu-Pa priests seem on the average to live much purer lives than do those of other sects in Tibet.

It is not only in the field of practice that Tson-Kha-Pa's contribution is outstanding. His original interpretation of the doctrine of "the Middle View," as founded by the Indian master, Nagarjuna, in the second century is also considered a great achievement by the Ge-Lu-Pa. The Middle View means a middle course between the extreme views of affirmation and negation of existence. Though a full elaboration of the theory is beyond our purpose and ability, yet we may obtain a glimpse of it through the favorite and apt illustration of an army.

It is reasoned that as long as an army is in operation, it has a commander in chief, with the rank and file and the elaborate organization that makes an army. It can attack and defend and serve all the purposes of an army. Once it is demobilized, however, everyone in the army returns to his individual pursuits, and the institution and function of an army disappear. Thus, in an ultimate and supreme sense, an army as such never exists; while in a non-ultimate and conventional sense, it does. This is the Middle View which forms the basis of the Ge-Lu-Pa's theory of "the Voidness." It is one of the five required courses in all the leading lamaseries of the Ge-Lu-Pa.

To an average observer, however, it is in monastic and clerical organization, rather than in anything else, that the Ge-Lu-Pa excels all the other sects. At the apex is the Dalai Lama, the religious-political head of Tibet in the Potala. Immediately below him is the triumvirate of the Dre-Pung, Se-Ra, and Gan-Dan monasteries. The triumvirate not only forms the economic and cultural backbone of the Ge-Lu-Pa sect, but also wields, through its wide ramifications throughout the country, a determining influence on the political and religious life of Tibet. Politically, only the three monasteries of Dre-Pung, Se-Ra, and Gan-Dan are entitled to represent the clergy in the national conferences summoned on important occasions. They own a large amount of real estate, which, in feudal Tibet, amounts to almost regional governments; they run a few magistracies with full administrative authority; and they supply the rank and file of the clerical staff, who, together with the lay nobility, are jointly responsible for the Tibetan government. Religiously, they have innumerable affiliated monasteries of varying sizes all over Tibet, and they offer degrees which are recognized and respected wherever Lamaism is practiced. With few exceptions, all the lama dignitaries, including the so-called incarnations of gods, must belong to one of the three monasteries in order to win public recognition. Even the Dalai Lama himself belongs to them all. Whenever a young Dalai Lama comes of age, a most important function before he assumes religio-political authority is his visit to the three monasteries, to be enrolled as a member of each congregation, starting always from his alma mater, Dre-Pung.

Dre-Pung is no doubt the most powerful of the triumvirate today. With a total congregation of seventy-seven hundred lamas, it is renowned as one of the largest monasteries, if not the largest, in the world. Se-Ra has a congregation of fifty-five hundred; and Gan-Dan, thirty-three hundred. These figures, which have gained a proverbial currency, are not to be taken too literally.

Theoretically, Gan-Dan, the smallest of the three, is still recognized as the fountainhead of the Ge-Lu-Pa. It claims as affiliated institutions the two famous academies for occultist studies in Lhasa, namely Gyu-Me and Gyu-To. Both these academies were founded by the direct disciples of Tson-Kha-Pa for the advanced learning of Tantra. The scholars to be admitted there are graduates from the triumvirate with a degree called Ge-Shi (Friend to Virtue). A Ge-Shi is supposed to have mastered all the exoteric studies, and is, in accordance with certain Buddhist theorists, qualified to take up the esoteric course. The twin academies of Gyu-Me and Gyu-To form thus a sort of postgraduate school, and from among their graduates come the candidates for the highest honor of the Ge-Lu-Pa order. A throne (Khri) in the Gan-Dan monastery, said to be the one on which Tson-Kha-Pa sat, is preserved to this day for the best scholar of the sect. The occupant of the throne is known as Gan-Dan Khri-Pa (the Enthroned of Gan-Dan) and is recognized as the legitimate successor of the great founder himself. It is the Gan-Dan Khri-Pa rather than the Dalai Lama who should be the real pope of the Ge-Lu-Pa sect. Only the senior of the graduates of the two academies can aspire to occupy the throne.

Added to this inner constellation around the Dalai Lama are a private church of his in the Potala and a curious temple named Nai-Ch'ung (Small Place) at the foot of the Dre-Pung monastery. The chief function of the private church is to pray for long life of the Dalai incarnation. The function of the temple Nai-Ch'ung is to give oracles. "Nai-Ch'ung" has also become the nickname of the god of oracle enshrined in the temple. Originally a guardian diety of the Dre-Pung monastery, the god has become, along with the Dalai Lama's ascendancy, the state oracle of Tibet. The Nai-Ch'ung oracle, like all other oracles in Tibet, gives prophecies through a human medium, who is always a monk in the temple and occupies a high government rank. Regularly, the Tibetan government sends representatives to the oracle to seek advice. In emergencies, even the Dalai Lama or the regent goes for help.

The Dalai Lama with his private church, the triumvirate of Dre-Pung, Se-Ra, and Gan-Dan, the two esoteric academies of Gyu-Me and Gyu-To, and the oracle of Nai-Ch'ung form the nucleus of the Ge-Lu-Pa organization. Tibetans refer to them as the Seven Great Symbols.

The other pillar of the Ge-Lu-Pa, the Panchen Lama, with his Tra-Shi Lun-Po monastery at Shigatse, maintains a court and a separate monastic organization exactly like those of the Dalai Lama but on a much smaller scale. Though also tracing its origin to the reformer, Tson-Kha-Pa, Tra-Shi Lun-Po cherishes a tradition of its own. Just as the Dalai Lama is surrounded by the Three Seats of Learning, the Panchen Lama is the center of his Lamas of the Four Quarters, meaning the abbots of the four colleges of Tra-Shi Lun-Po. Like the position of the Gan-Dan Khri-Pa, who is the head of the esoteric and exoteric congregations under the Dalai Lama, the culmination of the career of a lama in Tra-Shi Lun-Po, after decades of exoteric and esoteric training, is to become the Great Precious Master of Occultism (Nga-Ch'en Rin-Po-Ch'e). Tra-Shi Lun-Po also has its own oracle, its own affiliated institutions, and its own textbooks and degrees. However, since the exile of the late Panchen Lama in 1924, Tra-Shi Lun-Po was put under the direct control of the Lhasa authority. Now, with the return of the Tenth Panchen Lama, Tra-Shi Lun-Po seems to be once more in a state of change. Therefore, in the following pages only the institutions of the Dalai Lama will be discussed as examples of Tibetan monastic organization.

## Inside the Lamaseries

The best way to get a picture of the lamaseries and lama communities of contemporary Tibet is to draw an analogy between the three leading lamaseries of Dre-Pung, Se-Ra, and Gan-Dan and modern Western institutions of learning. Though such an analogy can be easily overdone, yet it still remains the best analogy.

Each of these lamaseries is built on a three-layer organization of La-Chi (the university board), Dra-Tshang (the college), and Kham-Tshen (somewhat like the dormitory). Forming the backbone of the institution is the middle layer, Dra-Tshang. Like a college in a modern university, it forms a compact, self-contained administrative unit, financially and academically. Besides keeping its own property, real estate, and revenues, a Dra-Tshang retains a high degree of autonomy in its curriculum, textbooks, and rule of discipline. Both of the esoteric academies, Gyu-Me and Gyu-To, are independent Dra-Tshangs.

Forming the center of all activities in a Dra-Tshang is the prayer hall, which is also the location of an administrative committee under the chairmanship of a Khen-Po, who is, in our analogy, the college president. In government-financed institutions, like Dre-Pung, Se-Ra, and Gan-Dan, a Khen-Po is first elected from among graduates with the Ge-Shi degree of the college concerned and is then chosen by the Dalai Lama or the regent from several such candidates, for a term of six to seven years. Besides representing the Dra-Tshang in all its external relations, a Khen-Po appoints committee members to assist him in the internal administration. Allowing for certain minor differences in such committees, the most important members are: first, the steward in charge of general affairs, including finance; second, the choir leader, somewhat like a dean; and third, the proctor. All have definite terms of office. The teaching staff does not figure in the faculty. The fact is that in a lamasery a teaching staff, as such, does not exist. Aside from certain hints the Khen-Po gives during class hour, a lama student is left to himself to find a tutor or any number of tutors he can afford. Study is not obligatory. There is even a name for those who do study, "the Book Man" (Bai-Ch'a-Wa)—as distinct from the ordinary monks, who constitute perhaps three-fourths of the total congregation.

To such student lamas the Khen-Po gives his regular lessons in a sort of garden, often with a small grove. This open-air classroom is the center for group studies. Besides the Khen-Po's short lecture, the students practice their theological debates there with much noise and dramatic display.

A smaller constituent unit under a Dra-Tshang, organized on a similar pattern, is the Kham-Tshen. It is, however, built on a regional basis. Monks from certain geographical or linguistic areas are enrolled in certain Kham-Tshens according to tradition. Such tradition, once established, cannot be changed without serious dispute. A Kham-Tshen, too, is a self-contained financial unit. It does not share its resources with other Kham-Tshens, though it does share equally the revenues accrued in the common treasury of its Dra-Tshang.

Such a Kham-Tshen also has a prayer hall, surrounded by the dormitories of all its members. The committee that runs it is elected by members of the

Kham-Tshen according to seniority, and is under the chairmanship of a senior of seniors. Serving under him are several seniors. The position of such a senior entails much responsibility without reward, and hence is obligatory for every newcomer by rotation. Those who are not willing to serve in the posts have to pay a stipulated amount of exemption fee. A small Dra-Tshang may have no Kham-Tshen under it; but the largest Dra-Tshang, which is in Dre-Pung monastery, is composed of twenty-three Kham-Tshens. Because of its financial independence, a Kham-Tshen may sometimes be better off than the Dra-Tshang to which it belongs. Such a prosperous Kham-Tshen may comprise a large number of smaller units modeled on itself. However, big or small, a Kham-Tshen is subject to a Dra-Tshang in its curriculum, discipline, and other matters, except those of finance.

Over all the independent Dra-Tshang organizations is a La-Chi committee for the whole lamasery, which functions in the great assembly hall known as Tsho-Ch'en. Usually built at the center of the lamasery, the great assembly hall is always the most splendid piece of architecture in a lama town, capable of accommodating thousands of monks and fronting on a spacious flagstone court with two towering flagpoles. As the name indicates, this is the place where the whole congregation of the lamasery assembles for its regular functions.

The La-Chi committee is composed of the Khen-Pos, who are the current presidents of all the Dra-Tshang units in the lamasery, under the chairmanship of the senior Khen-Po. The rest of the committee comprises all the counterparts of a Dra-Tshang committee but with different titles. Because of the importance attached to these functionaries, they are first nominated by the lamasery and then appointed for definite terms by the Dalai Lama or his regent.

Besides the three committees responsible for routine affairs, there is also a sort of legislative conference which may be convened on the three levels of Kham-Tshen, Dra-Tshang, or La-Chi to decide urgent matters. To be qualified to sit on the Kham-Tshen conference, one must have served the full term of a senior or paid the exemption fee. The Dra-Tshang conference is summoned by the Khen-Po and is attended by the representatives of all the constituent Kham-Tshens and by all holders of the Ge-Shi degree. Similarly, the La-Chi conference, which is summoned by the La-Chi committee, is attended by the representatives of all the Dra-Tshangs. If there are disagreements, the final authority is, of course, the Dalai Lama or his regent.

We have said that a lamasery at each of the three levels of organization forms an independent economic unit. All property of a lamasery, both from governmental and from private endowments, is divided accordingly. Governmental endowments may include subsidies in kind, funds, real estate, and even magistrate districts; private endowments include alms and donations in money and in kind from members of the congregation or from outsiders. To this we must add interest and dividends on banking and trading operations, in which all the lamaseries freely engage. This divided ownership of property is the reason so much is made of the traditional regional groupings. A member coming from a noble and rich family or from a large monastery with financial backing is an asset to all in the same unit.

To be a functionary on any of the three committees of La-Chi, Dra-Tshang, and Kham-Tshen is to become literally a "stuffed shirt." All Tibetans, including monks, are fond of pomp. Thus every one of the committee members wears a thickly padded vest under his robe in order to look larger. But the greatest stuffed shirt of all lama stuffed shirts is the head proctor. Each lamasery has two of these officers. They are dressed in vests that almost double their size, and they strut about in thick-soled boots. Each head proctor wields a richly wrought, square iron rod about three feet high, coated with gold and silver, and ending in a colorful tassel. This is the emblem of his absolute authority and justice. His mere appearance, as heralded by his emblem bearer, is enough to send the monks to the winds. Those who fail to run await him with protruding tongue, and bowing to the dust. To assist him in keeping order, each head proctor maintains a large retinue of lama "muscle men," including one who is accoutered exactly like a head proctor, even carrying an iron rod.

Among the proctors of the various lamaseries, those of the Dre-Pung monastery are the most powerful. During the Tibetan New Year, when more than twenty thousand monks flock to Lhasa to take part in the Great Prayer, the two head proctors of Dre-Pung become wardens of the law for Lhasa, controlling the religious and the lay communities. Their public appearance amidst all the pomp and fanfare of their large followings is a spectacle to which the Tibetans rush, even at the price of getting an occasional whipping.

## Enrollment and Progress of a Lama

Monks of all description flock to the lamaseries, some for education, some for social standing, some for vocational training, and some because they have nowhere else to go. A lamasery is a society in itself, wholly male in the case of the Ge-Lu-Pa, that permits all individual pursuits, provided that certain basic concepts of Buddhism are not transgressed. Each is a humming, growing town with a mass of many-storied buildings and a maze of narrow lanes. A distant view of its whitewashed and multiwindowed façade has reminded many European travelers of some large modern hotel on the Riviera.

Theoretically, the door of a lamasery is open to all. No age limit and no academic qualifications are set for entrance. Candidates from the age of five or six to fifty or sixty, scholars and illiterates, sons of the rich and the poor, as well as sons of the noble and of the nobodies, are all admitted on an equal footing, at least in theory. A lama of the Ge-Lu-Pa sect, even one who is supposed to be the incarnation of a god, must be enrolled and confirmed in one of the triumvirate before he gains public recognition.

To gain admission to such a lamasery, one must find a guarantor; the latter should already be a member of the lamasery and is supposed to assume unlimited responsibility for the applicant and see to his good conduct. A word from the Khen-Po is enough. Once admitted, the newcomer shaves his head and buys a uniform, which consists principally of an apron, a short vest, a long winding cloth, all of maroon wool, and a pair of pointed, upturned, skin boots. Thus rigged out, he is led to his dormitory at the Kam-Tshen to which he is assigned, enrolled on the list kept by the proctor of the Dra-Tshang, and then considered a member of the community.

As a member, he not only pays nothing to the lamasery but is entitled to a share of the allowance, in kind and in cash, from the three levels of the lamasery. In return, he owes to all of the three levels a service called *Khrai* (conscript labor or service). It summarizes all the obligations a Tibetan owes to his superior, whether that superior is a person or a legal body. A lama's Khrai to a lamasery may be serving tea to the congregation in assembly time, doing manual labor, or serving in unremunerative posts on the various committees. Competition for the lucrative positions is so strong that they are sold to the highest bidder. Bribery, as all who know Tibet will agree, is not regarded there as a serious offense. At the same time, a Khrai can be bought off with money. With money there is always "free" labor available for any kind of job.

But the better way to get exemption from Khrai is by subscribing to a privileged status. To an incarnation lama, that is, a lama who is supposed to be the incarnation of a god in this world, such a status is an obvious necessity. In fact nobody can become an incarnation lama until, by a prescribed process, he gains recognition by the congregation. The process consists first of a formal application to the Dalai Lama. The secretariat of the Dalai Lama keeps a list of such incarnation lamas and grants to each the rank which belongs to him. Generally speaking, there are two chief ranks, namely Tsho-Ch'en incarnations and Dra-Tshang incarnations. Once the application is approved, the incarnation must stand host once to the congregation of the whole lamasery or Dra-Tshang, according to his rank, serving tea and cooked rice to all, besides giving alms or making donations. The occasion also is celebrated with gift giving and feasting. After that, the incarnation lama is immediately promoted to a seat of honor in keeping with his rank in the great assembly hall, as well as in the halls of his Dra-Tshang and Kham-Tshen. Then he is officially recognized as an incarnation lama. To gain official recognition in one of the triumvirate of Dre-Pung, Se-Ra, and Gan-Dan is to gain official recognition all over Tibet. This is the first aim of an incarnation lama, the exemption from Khrai being a matter of course. Once recognized as an incarnation, he will be respected and honored in strict accordance with his rank wherever he goes. All the greatest incarnation lamas of the Ge-Lu-Pa sect, including those qualified to be the Dalai Lama's regent, belong to the rank of Tsho-Ch'en.

However, not everyone can be an incarnation. Therefore, by a somewhat similar process, any ordinary monk with enough resources many apply for another privileged status called *Ch'on-Dse*. A Ch'on-Dse status may be applied for on the three levels of Tsho-Ch'en, Dra-Tshang, and Kham-Tshen, with corresponding scales of investment and returns.

The holder of a privileged status is entitled to various advantages, one of which is the shortening of the academic term by four or five years. Thus, even economically speaking, this status pays. The reason given for granting such an advantage is that, since a privileged monk is exempted from all services and has more time to devote to his studies, he should be allowed to complete his course earlier.

Considering the size of the congregations in the three lamaseries and the profuse demands for gifts, the total investment for a special status would usually run to an enormous sum, far above the means of an average monk. One wonders to what extent this system is a cause or an effect of the general degeneration of the lamaist hierarchy, a tendency deplored by the more enlightened Tibetans themselves.


## A Lamaist Curriculum

It is worth repeating that in a lamasery there are lamas who study and lamas who do not. Among the latter group are those who are trained in all aspects of the religious rites which cater to the daily needs of the populace; those who specialize in vocal training; those with business talents, who manage monastic properties or carry on trading; artists—calligraphers and craftsmen; and all sorts of nondescripts, ranging from servants or mere hangers-on to the so-called lama warriors.

The Tibetan name for the lama warriors (Do Tho) means "villains," and villains, in the current sense of the word, they certainly are. Nearly all are illiterate and form somewhat of an outcast class in the lama community; they are often looked on with mixed scorn and dread in both monastic and secular circles.

No one seems to have pried into the origin of this queer class of lama warriors; and yet their organization bears marks of a long tradition and is to be found in all the more important lamaseries today. Of all lamas of the Ge-Lu-Pa sect, only the warriors are allowed to grow hair. And not only do they grow it, but they often wear it bobbed and curled as girls do. Their pleated aprons are of two layers, the outer layer being much shorter than the other. By using a specially cultivated and frivolous gait, the lama warriors make their aprons sway as they walk. They have a cult of their own. They worship their own gods; they chant their own hymns; and they cultivate among themselves a special *esprit de corps*, the main attributes of which are said to be unquestioned loyalty to their seniors and devotion to their comrades. They keep the utmost secrecy about the practices and organization of their cult. Every day they rise before dawn, bathe in cold water (which is no little feat in a Tibetan winter), and carry on vigorous gymnastics, like wrestling, stone throwing, running, broad jumping, and sword play. Most of them are the "hewers of wood and drawers of water." The senior members constitute a reserve from which the lama proctors draw their troops of henchmen. On festive occasions, and especially at the Tibetan New Year, these bullying, swaggering lamas appear in gala dress, with swords, whips, and sticks to maintain public order. In times of emergency a little inducement is enough to set them on an adventure at which a common monk would demur. They protect the premises against intrusion, accompany trade caravans, and serve as bodyguards to high lamas when traveling. Hence, their existence is indispensable to a lamasery. And if they have any ambition, it is to become proctors some day, especially proctors of the Dre-Pung monastery, whom they all idolize.

Except for the student lamas, the relation between the nonstudying community and the lamasery is more economic than religious. The nonstudying members are so free in their comings and goings that a good proportion of them are permanently or semipermanently absent. Even the lamas who are trained in all Buddhist rituals and services do not care much about the meaning of the scriptures, while most of the nonstudying community are illiterate. This is the case with all lamaseries, large or small, a fact that surprises foreign visitors.

Only before the student lama, the Bai-Ch'a-Wa, lies a real ecclesiastical career. But here at once is the dividing line between the two wings of the lamaist hierarchy. On the one hand is the hierarchy by birth—that is, the incarnation lamas from the Dalai Lama on down, who claim to have descended from the realm of gods or deities for the benefit of others. They, as a rule, are to be classified as akin to the student lamas, though being incarnation lamas they seldom have the time or patience to finish their academic course. On the other hand is the hierarchy by acquirement, to which those who claim no superhuman descent aspire. It is the career for all student lamas.

Because of the lack of any age limit or scholastic qualifications for admission, a new student invariably starts with a preparatory course in the Tibetan ABC's. Since there is no teaching faculty, he must find his own teacher from among the senior members and pay an amount of tuition, mostly in kind, such as is appropriate to the teacher's standing. A recommendation to the Khen-Po by the private tutor is enough to secure the new student's promotion to the regular class. For the illiterates or child students, this preparatory course may last five or six years, while for those who have already covered sufficient ground in language and religion, a few weeks may be enough.

Once enrolled in the regular class, the scholar steps on an ascending escalator, so to speak, wherein a yearly advancement becomes automatic. If a student, after completing his first year, were to be absent from the lamasery for three years, he would, on his return, be sent to the fifth class. There are altogether fifteen to sixteen classes, each with a different name. During class hours, each class is assigned a location in the open-air classroom by the proctor. Once a year, the proctor herds them over to the next place in order. Once the student reaches the last class, he becomes qualified to sit for the Ge-Shi examination. But to become a Ge-Shi costs money because of presents, feasting, and offerings to the whole Dra-Tshang congregation. Thus many leave without taking a degree, and even more leave without reaching the last class. To those with a privileged status, Ge-Shi examinations are granted five or six years earlier than they are to others. Since failure in the examinations is unheard of, it used to be customary for such students to leave the lamasery several years before finishing the full course.

All the leading Ge-Lu-Pa lamaseries offer five fundamental courses, each requiring two to five years for completion. Though the texts and the order of courses may vary from institution to institution, the subjects invariably include dialectics, disciplinary rules, and the Middle View.

A day's routine for a student lama begins with prayer at daybreak in the great assembly hall. Everyone is expected to attend. Into the many-pillared, gloomy interior file monks through its different doors, under supervision of the proctors and their assistants. Each monk finds his own position on a long strip of Tibetan wool carpet. On such occasions he wears a copious maroon cape in addition to the regular uniform. Those of the senior classes wear a yellow hat not unlike a vertical buffalo horn trimmed with fluffy wool along the inner curve. The students seat themselves Buddha-fashion, shoulder to shoulder and back to back, in long crisscross rows, filling every corner and niche, but leaving narrow lanes between them. High raised seats along the upper end of the hall are reserved for Khen-Pos and ex-Khen-Pos, who, like the row of gilt Buddhas behind them, look down upon the whole congregation. Squatting on a dais before them is the choir leader. The service consists of chanting hymns, with regular intermissions for tea. The singing of psalms is a great art in Tibet. It is done in a deep bass devoid of any element of melody but full of changes in tempo and volume. The single voice of the choir leader sounds not unlike the throbbing of a distant engine. When thousands of such voices join in, with an occasional clapping of thousands of hands to mark the stanzas, it is like the distant roar of the sea, with the sporadic dashing of breakers on the rocks. It is an art that requires years of training, and is practiced day and night in the desolate valleys and hills. Nothing is more suggestive of the weirdness and uncanniness of Tibet.

During the intermissions, tea—the famous, strong-smelling, salty, buttered tea of Tibet—is served in big pots to the whole congregation by the "freshman" monks. Everyone whips out a small wooden bowl from his pouch and holds it forth to receive the ration. Each morning three to four bowls of such tea are given gratis. At the last bowl, a monk produces his bag of barley meal (*Tsam-Pa*), and after pouring some of the parched barley powder into the tea, he kneads the mixture into small solid balls, which he pops into his mouth. This is his breakfast.

All this is done under the supervision of the proctors, who chide sternly, and if necessary promptly employ their big sticks. This morning tea is one form of government subsidy. The amounts of butter, tea, salt, and soda used in the beverage are measured according to age-old rules, and the preparation is supervised by a special officer. The cauldron used for making the tea may measure nine feet in diameter and four feet in depth; and dozens of people are employed to do the cooking. There is a standing joke that occasionally one of these cooks topples over into the seething cauldron and disappears without anybody's noticing it.

After the morning service, the monks retire to the halls of their several Kham-Tshens, where they sit in rows and chant in the same fashion as in the morning service. Then the students attend open-air classes. They sit on the ground, each class forming a group. When the Khen-Po arrives and takes his seat on a platform, the groups in turn crouch before him to hear their lessons. He gives a few succinct sentences in a hushed tone and then waves them away for the next class. Thus each class comes before him, under the supervision of the proctor with his big stick. While one class is receiving instructions, the rest form circles and practice debating.

The Ge-Lu-Pa attaches great importance to these open debates. In the more popular form of debate, there is one challenged person who defends a question against any number of challengers. One of the challengers raises the question, putting it in such a way that a yes-or-no answer enables the defender to state his position. Once this answer is given, the challenger pounds the defender with one question after another, framing his questions according to the defender's stated position, like a public prosecutor. The logic follows the strict formulas of Buddhist dialectics, and an apt quotation from the scriptures is always final. The defender remains seated throughout, and must give his answers in as succinct and composed a manner as possible; but any challenger is allowed full freedom in expression and movement, ejaculating, gesticulating, joking, and taunting, amid the general mirth of the audience. Not infrequently the affair becomes spirited when two or three challengers are active at once, or when one of the debaters is unable to continue. As we shall see, these debates are the only form of examination known to lamaist education, and hence are an absolute requirement for all who aspire to a degree.

After class, everyone assembles at the Kham-Tshen hall. Tea is then served by the Kham-Tshen authority, and most of the monks take their midday meal. The process is the same as in the morning assembly. Another chanting and debating lesson in the open-air classroom begins at five o'clock and lasts well into the evening. Occasionally, the students are treated to another free tea at the Dra-Tshang hall. To the poorer students free tea is a great help, and they subsist on little else. Those more fortunate, however, cook their own meals in their private cells. Many others employ cooks and servants, and live in lavishly appointed flats.

Lamaseries have something like a semester system, which divides each academic year in two. One semester starts after the New Year holidays, observed a little earlier than the lay Tibetan New Year. On this occasion, all the monks flock to Lhasa to join the Great Prayer. But before the New Year vacation, the students of Dre-Pung, Se-Ra, and Gan-Dan assemble at a place little more than one day's journey southwest of Lhasa. There a special course on dialectics is opened by a monastery affiliated with Dre-Pung for the benefit of all. The second term is separated from the first by a summer vacation of about one month. This is the time when all retire to the various hermitages in the neighborhood to meditate quietly on this transient and illusory life.


## Graduation and Afterward

Graduation, as we know it in a modern school, does not occur in a lamasery. After a student has advanced to the last class, which by a curious inversion is called the first class, he may stay there for life if he finds no other way out. However, he is qualified to apply for an examination for a Ge-Shi degree, which is tantamount to an academic degree in a university.

There are, altogether, four types of Ge-Shi degrees offered by Dre-Pung, Se-Ra, and Gan-Dan; two lower ones to be conferred by the lamaseries themselves and two higher ones to be given under government supervision. First of all, a qualified candidate should apply to the Khen-Po for permission to sit in the Ge-Shi examination, which is usually held after the summer vacation. The examination takes the form of a debate before the Khen-Po, in which five specially selected "seniors" one after another examine the candidate on subjects chosen extempore by the Khen-Po from the five principal courses. The Khen-Po also gives the final decision and assigns to each candidate whichever of the four classes of Ge-Shi he deems fit. Failure to pass seems unheard of. Tradition enjoins on every successful candidate the obligation to treat the whole congregation of his own Dra-Tshang and Kham-Tshen to tea and cooked rice and, if possible, to distribute alms. There are also an exchange of gifts and much feasting on such occasions, in which relatives and lay friends participate, as well as fellow monks. The total expenditure is considerable and presents an insurmountable obstacle to the less wealthy students.

The number of candidates for the two higher classes of Ge-Shi is fixed for each of the three lamaseries every year by the Tibetan government. In addition to the examination conducted by the Khen-Po, already described, candidates are required to sit for a second test at the Jewel Garden (Nor-Bu Ling-Ka), where the Dalai Lama holds his summer court, and for a third public examination at Lhasa during the New Year festivals. Two great religious services are held at Lhasa during the Tibetan New Year. The first is called the Great Prayer (*Mon-Lam Ch'en-Po*), and the second, the Assembly Service (*Tshom-Ch'o*). Those who take their public examinations during the Great Prayer are first-class Ge-Shis, while those who take their examinations in the Assembly Service are second-class Ge-Shis. Each of these two classes is assigned to defend the truth one day in the Central Cathedral of Lhasa, where anybody may go to engage him in this intellectual fencing.

So far, we have followed the career of the student lama from his matriculation to his graduation with a degree. Now he has reached the zenith of his career in the exoteric course. But there still lies before him a full course of occulist studies, provided he aspires to higher honors. Here is one of the basic contentions among Buddhists—the respective merits and order of the exoteric and the esoteric learnings. One school of opinion, to which the Ge-Lu-Pa sect subscribes, says that the proper way for an average votary to attain Buddhahood is to start with the exoteric and go on to the esoteric training—to proceed from the "know why" into the "know how." A Ge-Shi, who is already the master of the exoteric studies, must enter one of the twin academies of Gyu-Me and Gyu-To to climb to the very peak of a lamaist career.

The people of Tibet cherish a tender affection for the lamas of the two occultist academies. Both academies are famous for solid learning, discipline, and ascetic training. They offer no privileged status to anybody, not even to the incarnation lamas, who, consequently, seldom venture there. The disciplinary rules of these academies cover all fields of daily living, including dress and eating and sleeping, as well as certain conduct which is enshrouded in deep mystery and is suitable only for a congregation of the initiated.

Scholars in these two academies study Yoga, which is said to belong to an elevated physical-spiritual field which common mortals can never hope to experience. They have a unique master-disciple tradition and countless rituals and symbolisms that make fun of our common sense. Their training comprises an elaborate program of exercises to achieve complete mastery of all the spiritual and physical forces and thus effects a union of the individual self (the finite) with the universal self (the infinite). Each lama picks one favorite god as his ideal and learns to recast his own personality, amid certain appropriate surroundings, to attain unity with him. But one look at many of these occultist gods or goddesses is always enough to shock the layman's esthetic or moral sense. The graduates of the academies are selected by the Dalai Lama to serve on the faculties; and from those who have served a full term of Khen-Po in the academies come the candidates for the pope of Ge-Lu-Pa, the Gan-Dan Khri-Pa.

One interesting feature in the education of these esoteric scholars is that they spend considerably more time roaming about Lhasa and its environs than they do in their own academies. Each of the two academies follows a definite itinerary from Lhasa to points two or three days' journey away. During such travels, every scholar carries his belongings and walks the whole distance. Only the Khen-Po is privileged to ride. Thus do they follow the same itinerary every year, like two planets in a constellation, and meet only once in the Gan-Dan monastery, to which they are in theory affiliated. Then the Khen-Po of each academy asks leave of the head proctor of Gan-Dan for absence of his staff and student body from their alma mater during the current year.


## The Lamaist Hierarchies

Tibetans, like the ancient Greeks, not only humanize their gods but also deify human beings. For Tibetans, the world is full of visitors from other worlds. Nor do they find strange the possibility of daily contacts with incarnations of Buddhas and lesser deities. They consider this world as merely one step on the ladder up and down which all forms of mind-possessors from Buddhas to the dwellers in Hell are voluntarily or involuntarily climbing. Thus do Tibetans worship equally gods who have come down to save men and men who are going up to the kingdom of the gods.

Because of such beliefs, the lamaist hierarchy consists of two branches which it is convenient to call the hierarchy by birth and the hierarchy by acquirement.

As for the hierarchy by acquirement, when an average Ge-Shi enters the esoteric academies, he is entering an unlimited term of apprenticeship with no prospect of a higher degree. Most Ge-Shis, therefore, leave after a certain number of years to continue studies by themselves or to become respected members in some lamasery. For the holders of the first-class Ge-Shi degree, however, there is the chance of promotion, in the order of seniority in enrollment, to the faculty of the academies. Whenever vacancies occur, the senior among the first-class Ge-Shis may be promoted. He may thus be promoted up to the position of Khen-Po. After he has served the full term as a Khen-Po he retires, and his name is included in a special list. The seniors on the lists of both academies are known as Deans of Law, who are the alternate successors to the Ge-Lu-Pa papacy, the Gan-Dan Khri-Pa.

The Gan-Dan Khri-Pa and the two Deans of Law are regarded as the living symbols of the holy trio (Tson-Kha-Pa and his two greatest disciples), and are worshiped as gods, not in the sense of incarnations but as beings, once human, who have just achieved the status of gods in this life. By a rough computation, the career from a novice to these peaks of lamadom takes half a century—that is, barring accidents.

As for the hierarchy by birth, we do not know how many incarnation lamas there are in Tibet today. There must be hundreds with more or less pretentious claims, all professing to have descended from some higher realms. The secretariat of the Dalai Lama keeps a list of those who have won public recognition at the head of which are those qualified to be regents of Tibet. If we include in the list those who have not been accorded official recognition and the incarnation lamas of other sects, then the total number would be astounding. The superabundance of incarnation lamas in Tibet is a joke among the Tibetans themselves.

Many other lamaist hierarchies—the Sa-Kya family for instance—existed in Tibet long before that of Ge-Lu-Pa, and some still enjoy a large following. However, the Sa-Kya pontiff is succeeded, not by reincarnation, but by natural descent. Two lateral branches now compose the Sa-Kya family, and the head of each alternately succeeds to the throne for life. The sons of the families are allowed to marry and live like laymen, but the daughters are required to remain virgins.

A unique hierarchy in lamadom is the female incarnation, called "Queen-Sow, the Thunderbolt," at the famed Sam-Ding-Ling monastery, on a beautiful lake about two days' journey east of Gyantse. Supposedly the incarnation of a sow-goddess, about whom hangs a cluster of legends, she belongs to a subsect of Ka-Gyur-Pa, and once held a high diploma issued by the Chinese emperor. The only woman in all the incarnations of Tibet, she maintains a court and a monastery composed exclusively of males. This leads one to ask what position a woman holds in lamadom. In Lamaism, as well as in Buddhism, women are decidedly inferior to men. For a woman to attain Nirvana, it is said, she must be reborn a man first of all. Nuns and nunneries occupy an insignificant place in lamadom. However, worship of the female force is a common feature in the tantric school. There woman plays the role of an inferior but vital partner, technically known as a religious consort.

Just as it is difficult to prove a bona fide incarnation, it would be equally difficult to disprove it. Even the authority of the Dalai Lama cannot do much about the ever increasing number of incarnations. Some attempt of systematization has been made by the Lhasa government, and not infrequently one hears of the incarnation lamas being promoted, demoted, or deposed by the Dalai Lama. Of course, once it is admitted that these lamas are gods, all these doings can be accepted as the affairs of gods.

If, however, one were to view the institution of the incarnation lamas in a worldly light, then one would be tempted to say that it has come into being simply to perpetuate the various economic blocs which the incarnations serve as constitutional heads. Every incarnation lama represents certain vested interests from which a bloc derives its existence. A natural heir for a lama (at least for a Ge-Lu-Pa) being out of the question, the unique device of selecting a child as his successor is resorted to, in order to prevent internal dissension and preserve the legal body from breaking up.


## Temples and Oracles

Every lama temple presents the same, almost indescribable picture of moldy gloom and general confusion. With no pretense at arrangement, images of gods of all sizes are haphazardly put alongside miniature pagodas and mandalas (cosmic molds used in tantric liturgies) and sometimes before shelves of holy scriptures, which are rarely dusted. An imposing statue in a conspicuous position may be that of an incarnation lama or Khen-Po belonging to the lamasery; while the image of Sakya Muni himself may be stowed away in some dark corner. A tiny image may be considered especially holy because it once spoke. There are many talking images all over Tibet. There are rooms in which hundreds of miniature images are lined up behind wire screens and iron bars and tied by long strings to prevent pilfering. Occasionally you come upon a huge Buddha in a clean, light chamber which reminds you of a Chinese or Japanese temple. The next moment you are again in the dark. There are many interesting and rare objects in the lamasery. Yet they are not meant to be seen by human eyes but rather to be hidden in gloomy chambers and dark passages, behind drawn curtains and alongside steep and slippery staircases, through all of which you are led at a rapid pace. When you have been through a lamasery once or twice, you will find your curiosity more than satisfied. All lamaseries in Tibet look alike.

In all lamareries, large or small, there is one darkest chamber where no daylight is allowed to penetrate. That is the temple of the Guardian of the Law. The cult of the Guardian of the Law, the meeting ground of Bon-Po and Buddhism, is a thriving faith in Tibet. There are many strange things in the cult and many tales about its growth. The Tibetans believe that before the coming of the great occultist teacher, Padmasambhava, in the seventh century, Tibet was reigned over by a host of demons and demonesses. When Shanta-rakshita, the theologian who preceded Padmasambhava, started laying the foundations for Sam-Ye, the first Buddhist monastery of Tibet, the theologian was powerless against these evil deities, who nightly pulled down everything he built by day. Thereupon, Padmasambhava was invited to come to Tibet to chastize them. The demons and demonesses laid many traps for the

*Tibet and the Tibetans*

occultist master on his way from India through Nepal, but they were in turn conquered and converted into Buddhism to become the Guardians of the Law.

In the passage leading to the temples of these Guardians of the Law are always stuffed beasts—yaks, bears, and tigers—dangling from the ceiling, and old matchlocks, swords, spears, and shields are on the walls and pillars. A few carved or painted demonic deities guard the entrances, some of which are protected by heavy iron curtains with huge padlocks. Once you are inside, an usher with a flickering butter lamp and a hushed voice leads you to arrays of ferocious gods and goddesses whose very names he dares not pronounce; their features, hidden behind shrines, curtains, silk scarves, and veils, are more imagined than seen. Once or twice he moves his light near enough for you to get a glimpse of a glaring eye, a skull, the head of a hideous animal, or someone's feet trampling on bleeding human figures—all this in a dark, molding atmosphere laden with the smell of rancid butter offerings. Then before you can adjust your senses to their normal functions, you are hurried to the door, where the usher bows you out with the expression: "I have shown you all, you lucky one!" In some of these shrines, no women and children are allowed; if they were, the dreaded gods or goddesses might become angry.

Allied to this cult of the Guardians of the Law is the thriving trade of prophecy giving. Like Nai-Ch'ung, the guardian god of Dre-Pung monastery who became Tibet's state oracle, many other Guardians of the Law become oracles through whose human medium the Tibetan masses solicit guidance. There must be hundreds of such oracles operating all over Tibet, and many possess official standing. There are oracles of gods and goddesses, as well as oracles of demons and demonesses. There are oracles especially proficient in foretelling national events, and there are other oracles who are wiser in giving personal counsel. Some specialize in controlling the elements; others are famed for driving off evil spirits. Each of these oracles is run by a human medium. Some mediums are male, and some are female. Some are mediums for one god or goddess, and some for several. Some become hereditary in families and some in monasteries. Of those which are hereditary in a family, some are bequeathed only through the daughters and some only through the sons. Some of the gods possessing oracles are subordinate to other such gods; and some are sworn enemies of others.

There exists in Tibet today what must be one of the queerest celebrations in the world. Every twelfth year, in the Year of the Monkey, the state oracle, Nai-Ch'ung, acts as host for one day to all the major and minor oracles in and around Lhasa, inviting them to a banquet in the Nai-Ch'ung monastery. On that day, the image of the great teacher, Padmasambhava, is also welcomed there amid great ceremony from the Central Cathedral of Lhasa. All the mediums then work themselves into a trance, under supervision of Tibetan government representatives, and form a procession of gods and goddesses round the premises, followed by the host, also in a trance, and the image of the great teacher. They spend the rest of the day in revelry. This is in memory of the great teacher's conversion of them all to the cause of Buddhism. Among Tibetans the celebration is known as "an examination of the gods."

**part four**

*A Government of the God,
by the God, and
for the God*

## In Quest of God

When asked by a Tibetan friend to define democracy, we told him that it means a government of the people, by the people, and for the people. After some reflection, he commented: "Then, ours is a government of the god, by the god, and for the god."

The more one ponders on the Tibetan form of government, the more apt he is to admire the Tibetan genius for political adaptability. Apart from its apparent virtues for a credulous and unsophisticated populace, the Tibetan theocracy seems to be founded on the theory best calculated to minimize a somewhat unpleasant fact—Chinese overlordship. This overlordship sometimes meant effective sovereignty, when the Tibetan religious leaders relied on Chinese political and military power for unification and consolidation of their own position in Tibet as well as for defense against foreign invasion. Then Tibet hailed China as the great benefactor and protector; and Tibet was contented with a purely religious role, leaving its more worldly concerns to China. But sometimes, the Chinese overlordship came to mean only a nominal relationship, when China's power was in decline and when it merely held a tenuous suzerainty over Tibet. Then Tibet looked on China as a paying supporter to the religion of which Tibet was the exponent, and wanted to assert control over all its own affairs. In order to evolve a formula for such an elastic relationship with China, Tibet has tried to contain politics in religion by the theory of the chaplain-patron relationship. Thus, whether China's rule over Tibet is virtual or nominal, the term applied by Tibet to China has always been *Jin-Da* (Master or Patron). And, in either case, Tibet has regarded itself as supreme in religion, which to all Tibetans is a more primary concern than anything else. This concern is also shown by the fact that the capital city, which has remained the nerve center of Tibet for thirteen centuries and is now the residence of the Dalai Lama is called *Lhasa* (Land of God).

Granted that the Dalai Lama is the incarnation of Chen-Re-Zi, "the Compassionate," who has descended to Tibet to deliver all mind-possessors, it naturally follows that he should never die till his mission is completed, and hence, till then, there should be no question over his succession. Yet, conventionally speaking, he dies like all human beings when the human tabernacle in which he dwells reaches the stage of decay called death. As the Tibetans put it, he only "retires to the heavenly field." But true to the vow he made to deliver us, he returns again and again to continue his mission. When he returns, he takes a fresh human abode. How and where to find the Dalai Lama in his new incarnation is a major problem for the Tibetan science of divination.

In such a science there can be no fast rule to follow. Guidance is generally to be sought in three different stages before and after the passing of the old Dalai incarnation. First it is to be determined whether there were any indications before or at his passing as to when and where the savior would be reborn. Such indications are bound to be so apocalyptic that only a few highly initiated ones can understand them. A casual word or gesture from him, a line from his will or writing, the position in which he retires from this world, the objects he keeps around him at the last moment, as well as the way he keeps them—these may all be keys to the supreme riddle.

The cases of the Third, Sixth, and Thirteenth Dalai incarnations are famous. It is said that when the Third Dalai Lama neared his end in Mongolia, he was surrounded by Mongolian princes, who begged him to return among them to continue his spiritual ministration. The holy man assured them that he had the same wish in mind, and then expired. The next year

*Tibet and the Tibetans*

a son was born to the family of the Mongolian prince, Altan Khan, who was a patron of the Third Dalai Lama. The child was hailed as the fulfillment of the holy man's promise and was welcomed to Lhasa as the Fourth Dalai Lama. The romantic Sixth Dalai Lama, who would merrily have bartered his papacy for the heart of a Lhasa belle, left behind him over sixty lyrics of wine, women, and song. In one poem, he sang about the departure of a lover who promised an early return; in another, his poetic fancy rode on the wings of a crane to a place, in modern Sikang province, where the Third Dalai Lama founded a flourishing monastery. After the mysterious death of the lama-poet, when two rival candidates were put up as his successor, all Tibetans supported the pretender from Sikang because he fulfilled the veiled promise in the poems. The Thirteenth Dalai Lama is said to have expressed many times a desire to visit China in his last days. When he passed away in the sitting posture, in which all orthodox lamas sleep and die, he was found facing East. His successor, the present Dalai Lama, comes from China.

Determining the general compass direction in which to search does not, of course, provide a sufficient clue. The next step is to seek further evidence through oracles, drawing of lots, mathematical divination, and reading of visions. To invoke divine guidance, special services are organized in leading lamaseries, where prayers are continuously offered to "the Compassionate" to hasten his return. In short, the whole force of Tibetan prognostic science is mobilized under the direction of the lama divinities. Since all prophecies may not tally, greater weight is usually given to the state oracle of Nai-Ch'ung and particularly to the vision afforded by the famous lake, Lha-Mo Nam-Tso.

Many lakes exist in Tibet where, allegedly, one can read one's future. When appropriate prayers are offered, one sees on their calm surfaces scenes predicting events to come. But this lake, about five days' journey southeast of Lhasa, is especially noted as the favorite haunt of Pan-Dan Lha-Mo, the patron goddess of the Dalai Lama. Beside the lake is a temple where the image of the goddess is enshrined. The best time to visit the lake is said to be the fourth month of the Tibetan calendar (roughly, May), and the most auspicious day is the fifteenth of the month. On that day Tibetans offer sacrifices to appease the dragon-spirits of the world. The water then lies in perfect tranquillity, mirroring the secrets of the future.

When the new incarnation of the Dalai Lama is the secret to be learned, either the enthroned of the Gan-Dan monastery or the regent of Tibet comes to read the sign. After praying to Pan-Dan Lha-Mo for her divine guidance, he squats Buddha-fashion on the shore and contemplates the surface of the water for the vision to come. Sometimes it appears, but sometimes it does not. If not, the service is repeated the next day. The vision may take the form of a religious symbol, a Tibetan or Sanskrit letter, a human figure, a scene, or some other object. The seer dictates everything he sees to the scribe attending him. When his trance is over, he retires to his private quarters. There, amid constant invocations for divine guidance, he carefully considers his impressions and compares them with previous prophecies, until he has woven all the data into a coherent whole, giving the country and surroundings in which the new incarnation is to be found. This usually takes place four to five years after the passing of the previous incarnation. This delay is to give the new incarnation time to be born and reach early boyhood.

Scouting parties are then sent out with instructions based on the foregoing revelations. Every such party must be headed by one monk, often himself an incarnation lama, and one high-ranking lay officer. The two of them represent the religious and secular communities of Tibet. For their further guidance, the leaders of the party are instructed as to certain important physical marks or habits of the previous incarnation, and are given some of the latter's relics or articles of daily use, along with false ones. These articles are used to test the supposed incarnations. If a boy is the true incarnation, he should be able to tell the true relics from the false. Thus furnished, the party sets out into the wilds on this singular adventure of god-quest. The Tibetans call it "making the recognition."

After long rambling, the party may find a family resembling one described in the instructions. The leaders then go about in disguise to ascertain from the neighbors whether a boy lives there who was born in a certain year—the year after the passing of the former incarnation—and who is also noted for his extraordinary cleverness. If the leaders learn that there is such a boy, they go to visit him, variously disguising themselves. They may take with them actual relics of the previous incarnation as well as similar ones lacking that holy association, to see whether the boy can distinguish between them. The boy may show interest in the strangers or make friends with them. Perhaps he betrays certain manners or physical marks like those of the former Dalai Lama. He may even claim as his own a few of the former Dalai Lama's possessions! If he does so, the searchers believe that in him they have discovered the god's new bodily abode. A report is quickly submitted to Lhasa. The party now reveals its mission and waits till the invitation comes for the boy and his family to travel to Lhasa.

Such a mission sometimes takes two or three years to complete. Not infrequently more than one such discovery is made. The standing practice is to make a preliminary selection of three candidates, all of whom are invited to Lhasa. According to Buddhist theory, every being possesses three outlets of expression, namely, body, speech, and mind. Each of these may take a

*Mah-jongg is a favorite game of the Tibetans.*

*Interior of a Tibetan house. The walls and windows are elaborately decorated.*

*A Tibetan lady with her two stepdaughters*

*Arriving at a party.*

94

*Plowing time*

*Wine maids
in gala dress.*

Boy and girl of the urban people

Begging for alms—the
Tibetans are a
charitable people.

*Bar-Kor, Lhasa's main street, with vendors and stalls*

*He is a Yu Pa, or man of agriculture*

*Tibetan villager*

Convicts like these roam the streets of Lhasa

*A pilgrim
with his
prayer wheel.*

99

*Entrance to the house of a Tibetan noble*

separate incarnation. However, as both body and speech are believed to be governed by the mind, it is the "Incarnation of the Mind" who is considered the true incarnation. With a view to ending disputes at this stage and eliminating the growing practice of giving preference to candidates from powerful noble families, Emperor Chien-Lung in 1792 decreed the drawing of lots from a golden urn.

In accordance with that decree, the names of the rival candidates are written down on scrolls of paper, which are then put into barley-paste balls. The balls are put into a golden urn especially presented by the Emperor, which is sealed up and placed before the image of Sakya Muni in the Central Cathedral of Lhasa. After seven days of prayer, the Chinese resident Ambans go to the cathedral with the whole Tibetan court. After due ceremony, one of the Ambans picks up a paste ball with a pair of long ivory chopsticks and passes it to another official. The latter opens it and announces to the whole assemblage the name of the victorious candidate. All Lhasa then goes wild with acclamation, while the name of the new Dalai Lama is proclaimed from house to house and relayed by special announcements and messengers from place to place throughout Tibet and interior China.

However, it sometimes happens that when the various candidates are assembled in Lhasa, the claim of the true incarnation is so clearly established over his rivals that he is given the unanimous choice without the drawing of lots. Both the present Dalai Lama and his predecessor belong to this category. Nevertheless, one rule seems to have prevailed since Emperor Chien-Lung's decree, with the tacit approval of all Tibet. This is that a Dalai Lama must never come from a powerful noble family but always from humble stock.


## An Unwritten Constitution

Once the Dalai Lama with his superhuman claims is chosen, it is not difficult to set up something of a constitution for Tibet. As the incarnation of Bodhisattva (or Chen-Re-Zi, the Compassionate) he is the religious head of Tibet. And since, thanks to his patron, the Chinese emperor, he has acquired the greatest part of Tibet as a sort of endowment, he is also the political head of Tibet. In him is thus summed up the authority in Tibet for both the church and the state.

Tibet is a land dedicated to "the Law," as personified by the Dalai Lama. His possessions—the land and its people—are divided into two portions: first, the dominion of the church, and second, the dominion of the state. He assumes personal command of both. However, to assist him in governing, he has delegated his power over nonspiritual affairs to a government, named De-Pa-Zhung (Government of the Chief). On account of the Dalai Lama's dual role, such a government should represent equally both the religious and the secular communities of his domain, with precedence given to the former. In a land consecrated to Buddha, the secular community exists for the religious community and not vice versa. The state is contained within the church. For this reason, the chief of the administration should in principle always be a member of the holy order. He can be a layman only when the Dalai Lama is in personal charge of the government. During the absence of a Dalai Lama, such as the interim between his passing and the finding of a successor-incarnation as well as during the successor's years of minority, a regent should be elected from among the highest incarnation lamas of Tibet and invited to assume full responsibility of the government.

The regent may be appointed by the Dalai Lama himself before the latter's decease. If not, the regent is to be elected by a great national assembly summoned by the government for this special purpose. The candidate for the regency must be a first-class incarnation lama among the afore-mentioned Tsho-Ch'en incarnations of one of the three lamaseries, Dre-Pung, Se-Ra, and Gan-Dan. There are about half a dozen such qualified incarnations in the whole of Tibet. They are known as the "regal incarnations" from the fact that the regent of Tibet once bore the title of "King of Tibet." All the regal incarnations were created by the Chinese emperor and possessed diplomas issued by him. Their successor-incarnations, on attaining majority, have the first preference for the regency.

Also qualified to be regent of Tibet are the present and former occupants of the throne in the Gan-Dan monastery, i.e., the Gan-Dan Khri-Pa, as well as the Dalai Lama's preceptors. If the person elected regent is not the Gan-Dan Khri-Pa, he must in matters relating to religion consult and respect the latter in view of his authority as the successor of Tson-Kha-Pa. When the Dalai Lama attains his majority, between the ages of sixteen and eighteen, the regent surrenders to him all authority of the government. In the field of religion, only the Dalai Lama can share authority with the Gan-Dan Khri-Pa.

The prime duty of the government is concerned with the lay population of Tibet. All members of the holy order come within the direct authority of the church under the Dalai Lama and hence are beyond the immediate province of the government. As the interests of the ecclesiastical and secular communities are too closely bound to allow separate administration, the Dalai Lama appoints a rank and file of clerical officers, recruited from the three monasteries of Dre-Pung, Se-Ra, and Gan-Dan, to form a counterpart of the lay officers, who are recruited from the nobility. Thus constituted, the government is empowered to control all people in Tibet, religious and lay. However, even then the government's authority over the religious community extends only so far as is deemed fit by the Dalai Lama or his regent. The principle is that only a clergyman can exercise authority over the clergy.

In accordance with the rough division of Tibet into the dominion of the church and the dominion of the state, the Dalai Lama allots his land and people, together with their belongings, to three main groups. The first is the estate of the church, in which are also included all the properties granted to the individual lama dignitaries and the incarnations. The second is the estate of the state, to which all public properties belong. Such estates, together with their yields and returns, are mainly assigned to different offices in the government for their maintenance. The third division is the family estates. These fall into two groups. One group is made up of official feudal estates of the nobility, which are held by the male heirs of the families concerned, on the basis of one heir for one estate, and are not transferable. The other group includes the private holdings of the nobility and the small percentage owned by commoners who are subjects of the church, the state, or the nobility. Thus, all the land of Tibet must belong to one of the three groupings; and all the people of Tibet are also grouped according to the land from which a family derives its subsistence.

The Dalai Lama is the lord of all Tibet. The relation between the Dalai Lama and his people may be characterized as that between a Jin-Da (lord) and his Mi-Sairs (serfs). As a lord, he is to give all Tibetans protection and good government; while as his serfs, they owe him Khrai, which includes taxation and service. This Khrai is obligatory, whether it is in the form of taxation—in money or in kind, or of service of a general or contingent nature. It is calculated on the basis of the productivity of the land, or other corresponding substitutes, as owned by the church, the state, and the nobility. The obligations of the church and the state are obvious enough. The all-important Khrai for the nobility is to furnish one son, the heir apparent, from each feudal estate to the Dalai Lama for public service. This, like all other Khrais, cannot be waived, though on reasonable grounds and the payment of appropriate fees a temporary exemption may be granted.

The same reciprocal relationship between the lord and the serf should govern the relationship between the church, the various governmnt units, and the nobility on the one hand and the common people on the other. That is to say, the church, the government, and the nobility, while giving protection and government to their respective subjects, may also demand Khrai, in the form of taxes and services. A subject of the church and the nobility, therefore, is under the obligation of rendering Khrai both to his immediate master and to the government as the delegated authority of the Dalai Lama.

Basically, every Tibetan, under the paramountcy of the Dalai Lama, is either a subject of the church if he belongs to the holy order, or a subject of the state if he does not. A subject of the state may belong to the government directly, or indirectly through the nobility. While the church may have many lay subjects from its estates, the state and the nobility are allowed no control over anybody once he becomes a monk. The moment a Tibetan receives ordination, he, or she, as in the case of a nun, is subject only to the church and the Dalai Lama. For instance, a noble lord loses his serf when the latter is admitted into a monastery, and the lord may claim the serf back only with the permission of the monastery or when the serf is dismissed by the monastery. The power of the church is above all, for Tibet is a land of the god, by the god, and for the god, and every Tibetan is pledged to do reverence to the "Three Gems"—the Buddha, the Law, and the Priesthood.

## The Peak, the Lower, and the Assembly

The people of Lhasa refer to the Dalai Lama and his inner court as *Tse* (the Peak), a word that stands in many contexts as a synonym for the church, or religion. Here is not just a figure of speech, but a fact. Rising above the western suburb of Lhasa is a rocky hill on which stands the palace Potala, thirteen stories high, dominating the surrounding plain. The Dalai Lama maintains his court on the gold-roofed top floor, a living symbol of religion, the peak of everything Tibetan.

The name "Dalai Lama" is not used by the Tibetans. Among his many high-sounding titles favored by the Tibetans, the most popular are Bye-Wa Rin-Po-Ch'e (Precious Lord) and Kyam-Gon Rin-Po-Ch'e (Precious Savior). To see to his personal affairs and private properties, there is a Chi-Ch'ub Khen-Po (Lord Chamberlain), assisted by three lesser Khen-Pos, in charge, respectively, of the Dalai Lama's food, daily living, and religious ceremonials. The four are inseparable from him and accompany him wherever he goes. Collectively, the four men are known as the Khen-Pos of the Rear.

Responsible for the Dalai Lama's education are two preceptors who teach him scriptures and a number of assistants who practice with him the all-important religious disputation. All are recruited from the Ge-Lu-Pa triumvirate of the Dre-Pung, Se-Ra, and Gan-Dan monasteries, and the two preceptors are always first-class incarnation lamas. Though their chief concern is religion, their influence in molding the character, opinion, and conduct of affairs of His Holiness is tremendous. To complete this inner circle is a private secretariat, also staffed by the best talents from the above-mentioned triumvirate, and under the charge of the Chi-Ch'ub Khen-Po.

As the Dalai Lama, with his inner court, is not supposed to have any direct dealings with anybody, there is a liaison office called *Tse-Ga* (Front of the Peak) which acts as an intermediary between His Holiness and the outside world, including the Tibetan government. This office is in charge of the grand steward, a high lama officer, who is assisted by an exclusively clerical staff. Prominent on the staff are four awesome, gigantic lama bodyguards, who act as the Dalai Lama's heralds and police in public ceremonies. Especially picked for their stature, which they exaggerate with stuffed underclothing, each of these formidable lamas holds in one hand a string of beads and in the other a huge whip, with which he chastises any Tibetan on the slightest provocation.

Just below the Peak, geographically as well as figuratively, is *Shor* (the Lower), which is a synonym for secular Tibet. Shor, the starting point of the Tibetan government, may be either a clerical or secular organization. When the Dalai Lama is underage, the regent is the head of this administration. He maintains a small court of his own and also has a liaison office, known as the *Shor-Ga* (Front of the Lower). A regent takes the reins of the Tibetan government supposedly on the latter's invitation. Two special monk officers are appointed by the government to see to his private needs. He is commonly called Si-Chong Rin-Po-Ch'e (Precious Regent), in keeping with his status as an incarnation lama. And due to his being a clergyman, his liaison office is entirely staffed by the clergy. However, once the Dalai Lama assumes control of the government, the liaison office is turned into a purely lay organization, sometimes under a prime minister who comes from the top stratum of the nobility.

From Shor, the starting point, stem two parallel systems composed of the clerical and the secular officials. Putting in practice the principle of containing politics in religion, the clerical and secular systems run through the Tibetan administration from top to bottom. The highest office in the administration is a sort of cabinet, known as *Ka-Sha*, normally in the charge of four ministers. These ministers, of whom the leader must be clerical while the other three are secular, are jointly responsible to the Dalai Lama or his regent for the whole government of Tibet. Under the cabinet are the secretariat, the recruiting office of the clerical arm, jointly headed by four grand secretaries, all monk officers, and the secular counterpart, the finance office, jointly headed by four finance officers, all laymen. The cabinet and these two offices form the pivot of the government. In principle, the four grand secretaries are subordinate to the cabinet and on a par with the four finance officers. However, in matters of a purely or predominantly ecclesiastical nature, the grand secretaries can gain direct access to the Dalai Lama or his regent by going over the heads of the four ministers.

Before proceeding to analyze this parallel system of government in greater detail, it may be appropriate to discuss the so-called Tibetan parliament (*Tshom-Du*). This much-vaunted "democratic legislature" of Tibet is, on closer analysis, neither democratic nor a legislature. First of all, there is no regular session of the parliament, and both the agenda and the summoning are beyond the power of the constituent members. A conference is called by the order of the government to deal only with specific issues. The four cabinet ministers who are responsible for steering the government do not directly participate in the deliberations but sit apart in a secret chamber. They fix the number of participants on each occasion; and only those whom they invite may come. The invited include, on the ecclesiastical side, the representatives of the three monasteries, Dre-Pung, Se-Ra, and Gan-Dan, who are elected by their own congregations, and on the secular side a few senior members of the nobility and the officers in charge of more important government organs, all to be appointed by the cabinet ministers. The conference is presided over by a committee of eight, comprising the four grand secretaries and the four finance ministers. During the discussion, the eight persons frequently communicate with the cabinet ministers by chits and exchange written opinions among themselves. The main debate is always carried on between this committee of eight and the monastic representatives, who act as a sort of opposition. A motion is never put to a vote. Whenever the opposition is silenced, the motion is considered carried. The committee thereupon puts the resolution in writing and submits it by a special messenger to the cabinet ministers, who, acting collectively as they always do, transmit it to the Dalai Lama or the regent. When a resolution is not found acceptable, it may be given back to the assembly for further deliberation. Such an occasion seldom arises. The cabinet ministers and the committee of eight see that it does not. This assembly, therefore, is at its best a consultative body, and at its worst a forum where the government records in public its most important decisions.

Tradition states that there is sometimes a larger version of the assembly when representatives from all administrative units in Tibet are invited to attend. This happens perhaps once in a lifetime. When a resolution is passed there, it is said, not even the Dalai Lama may alter it. Be that as it may, the assembly illustrates a typical feature of Tibetan politics—a semblance of collective responsibility. The whole Tibetan government is founded on the concept of an equal responsibility of the clergy and the nobility. A great number of government offices are headed by committees, and important policy decisions are always carried in the name of the national assembly. The fact is that everybody wants to be in the background and no one is eager to shoulder the responsibility. "In dealing with the Tibetan officials," a friend once commented, "you get the feeling of playing a perpetual game of hide and seek. They are always hiding, and you are always seeking."

## Tse-Kor, the Ecclesiastical Court

*Tse-Kor* (court of the Peak, or ecclesiastical court) is composed of monk officials called *Tse-Drung* (courtiers of the Peak). Writers often confuse these monk officers, who are following a completely mundane career, with the bona fide lamas because of their resemblance in dress and their common observance of a lifelong celibacy. It is also a fact that every candidate for Tse-Drung must first of all be enrolled as a member of one of the congregations of Dre-Pung, Se-Ra, and Gan-Dan. However, apart from these superficial resemblances, the Tse-Drung are a class by themselves.

We are not sure how the unique institution of the ecclesiastical court came into being, but it is supposed to have taken definite shape during the time of the Fifth Dalai Lama. If we were allowed to hazard a guess, we should be tempted to trace it to an analogous institution in China—the centuries-old imperial examination for civil servants. When a new dynasty has been ushered in, the first few emperors have often had difficulties with the boisterous aristocracy who helped them to the throne. In order to hold them in check, the Chinese emperors found it wise to enlist the support of the commoners by admitting them to imperial service through public examination. By so doing, not only have new talents been absorbed from the different social strata in the interests of the government, but also a new and nonhereditary aristocracy has been created, an aristocracy of scholarship owing its direct allegiance to the emperor and thus counterpoising the old aristocracy of birth. The Fifth Dalai Lama came to political power partly through the support of certain secular leaders. In order to check these powerful families and to consolidate the monastic hold over the feudal lords, he may have borrowed the Chinese idea of creating a new and flexible aristocracy which would owe direct allegiance to himself. And what could have been more natural than for him to create it from the priesthood which would be bound to him in the name of religion?

A Tse-Drung enjoys every privilege of a monk, and yet he is not a monk.

He gets a share of all the subsidies and donations from the three levels of the monastery in which he is enrolled, like any of its inmates. But he never stays there; he is not bound by any of the monastic rules except the vow of celibacy, and he does not read the scriptures. He is put through a different course of training, and his calling is most pronouncedly of this world. He crops his hair and is ordained like a monk; he wears boots with finely woven cloth and gold threads like those of the high lamas, but he wears a sleeve coat underneath the winding robe instead of the lamaist waistcoat. Thus, but for the sleeves, he looks exactly like a high lama, with whom he is certainly often confused by the ignorant Tibetan masses.

In theory anybody can become a monk officer or Tse-Drung, just as anybody can become a monk—that is, anybody except the Tibetan "untouchables," like the smiths, butchers, fishermen, hunters, and undertakers. To become qualified, one must first become enrolled in one of the three leading monasteries and then serve an apprenticeship under a Tse-Drung. Since a Tse-Drung is not allowed to have natural issue, an apprentice usually becomes the heir to his master's career and property. Upon the master's recommendation, the apprentice may get admission to a training school, called *Tse-Lub-Dra* (Peak School). This school forms one part of the secretariat (Yi-Tshang) under the four grand secretaries who, apart from other duties, are responsible for the recruitment of the ecclesiastical officers. Any candidate eleven or twelve years old or more is eligible for admission. Once admitted to the school, he dons a uniform at government expense, composed of a dark red woolen gown, boots, and a flat scarlet hat with a wide brim, trimmed all around with short red tassels. He then goes through an unspecified period of grounding in calligraphy, grammar and rhetoric, and arithmetic while waiting for promotion to a subordinate position in the secretariat.

The secretariat is the only office under the cabinet staffed purely by clergymen. All affairs of the monastery, including discipline of the monks and registration of lama dignitaries of all sects, are in the charge of this office. The most complete record is kept there of all monastic organizations, with their respective numbers of inmates and properties, as well as of the whole lamaist hierarchy. But the secretariat draws its main prestige from the fact that it is the office of recruitment, training, and upkeep of the whole clerical staff in the ecclesiastical court, which by tradition is limited to one hundred seventy-five members.

Three times a year, the four grand secretaries recommend a list of senior students of the Peak School to the Dalai Lama or his regent for appointment as probationary officers in the ecclesiastical court. Those appointed change over to the full uniform of a Tse-Drung, and every morning attend a court tea before the Dalai Lama. This daily function is said to be modeled after the Chinese emperor's tradition of holding his court every morning to hear reports of his state affairs. These morning courts are held so early that they are said to be a check upon the ruler and his courtiers from falling into dissolute habits. In Tibet, this morning audience is called a "court tea" because every Tse-Drung, in the presence of the Dalai Lama, partakes of two bowls of tea and one bowl of congee, at government expense, as a reminder of his monastic days. All government appointments, promotions, demotions, transfers, and punishments are announced at this time. And this is also the time when the Dalai Lama grants audiences to visitors. No matter whether the Dalai Lama is residing at the Potala or at his summer palace or is traveling, the function is held daily, on a full or reduced scale, as conditions warrant. Even during the period between the passing of one Dalai Lama and the discovery of his successor, the function is held without interruption before his empty throne, on which his garment is arranged in a fashion suggesting his presence. It is no wonder that the ecclesiastical court is regarded as a court within the court and, unlike its secular counterpart, is considered semi-sacred.

One notices a better *esprit de corps* among the Tse-Drung than among the lay officials, who are always quarreling among themselves. With few exceptions, all the Tse-Drung rise from the lower social order and are self-made men. They generally display more enterprise and strength of character than their lay colleagues. And though looked upon by the nobility as social upstarts, they seem to carry more authority with the Tibetan masses, especially in the more remote regions where the aristocrats command little respect.

However, a few Tse-Drung come from the noblest families. They form a special class within the ecclesiastical court and enjoy an even higher prestige. It is interesting to see how the old aristocracy, the feudal lords, after losing ground to the new aristocracy of the Tse-Drung, manage to gain some compensation for their loss. Since a Tse-Drung is a member of the church, which is open to everybody, the church certainly cannot discriminate against members of the nobility, provided they are ready to renounce their secular status. Thus some sons of the noble families doff the silk gown and don a monk's robe. It is especially convenient to those noble families where there are sons to spare. For to have a son in the ecclesiastical arm of the government does not preclude the family's right, or obligation if you like, to have another in the secular arm. Such a privilege, however, is limited to a few, perhaps not more than a dozen families.

## Shor-Kor, the Secular Court

Just as Tse (the Peak) is the center of the ecclesiastical court, so Shor (the Lower) forms the center of the *Shor-Kor*, or secular court. The secular court is a monopoly of the nobility (Ku-Dra), of which there are perhaps one hundred fifty families left today. They are believed to be the descendants of kings, local chiefs, and their followers, who ruled Tibet in the old days. This figure, of course, does not take into account the members in lesser courts, of which there are still a number in Tibet, such as the courts of the Panchen Lama and the Sa-Kya pontiff. These families survived the change in Tibet when feudal chiefs were replaced by the lamaist hierarchy, and they have kept themselves in favor by giving allegiance to the lamaist regime.

It is futile to ask how much of the old blood is still running in the veins of a modern Tibetan aristocrat. Tibetans attach more importance to names than they do to blood. Besides, new families have been coming to replace those that have died out. A commoner with enough financial resources may apply and get appointed to a feudal estate for which there is no issue. The most obvious and prominent additions to the nobility are the families of the various Dalai incarnations. These families are recognized as nobility of the highest order. We know of at least five families who have been thus ennobled from the common stock.

Each noble family has, as a rule, one official fief from which it derives both its name and its existence. A family with an official fief has the duty of keeping one legitimate heir in service with the Dalai Lama at his secular court. A few families may have more than one official fief. In these cases, the fiefs are registered under different names, and for each a separate heir apparent is to be sent to the Dalai Lama's service. Should such an heir be unavailable or too young for service, the family must pay the government an exemption fee until the vacancy is filled. The full strength of the secular court is made to correspond to the ecclesiastical court, which, as we have seen already, is supposedly maintained within the limit of one hundred seventy-five members.

For these secular officials, or *Ku-Dra*, there also exists a training school, which is attached to the most important lay organization, the finance office (Tsi-Khang). Corresponding to the secretariat in the ecclesiastical arm, the finance office is starting point of an official career in the secular arm. It is under the joint charge of four finance officers, and has a purely lay staff. The most complete list of all official or private estates of the noble families and of the government is kept there.

The heir apparent of any noble family may be admitted to the training school of the finance office if he is between the ages of ten and twenty and has received some preliminary education. He is supposed to have mastered already the rudiments of a literary education essential for a son of the nobility, and his main study now is arithmetic. He puts on a uniform consisting of a dark woolen gown, with boots to match, and a queer yellow velvet hat like an upturned saucer. Dangling behind from his red silk waistband are a long scarlet brocade bag, a pair of smaller kidney-shaped embroidered pockets, and a cloisonné case holding a pair of ivory chopsticks and a penknife. This waistband, a curious mixture of Chinese and Tibetan fashions, has for some unaccountable reason become an emblem of all Tibetan government employees, high and low.

There are about twenty families among the noble class who enjoy an especially honorable position. The sons of these families are known as *Sai-Nam-Pa*. When a Sai-Nam-Pa enters the finance school, he is allowed to fasten a small, roundish metal amulet box onto his queue as a mark of honor. The Tibetan amulet box, always a beautiful object of art, is a necessity for both rich and poor; without it, a Tibetan will never undertake to do anything important. But while every Tibetan may carry an amulet box, only government officials of the fourth rank and above are allowed to wear it in their hair. Despite being juniors, the members of the Sai-Nam-Pa occupy in all public functions a place next below the fourth-rank government officers.

Tibetan arithmetic is a science said to have been perfected as late as the eighteenth century. It makes use of a counting machine composed of a wooden tray and a queer assortment of such objects as broken pieces of china, little twigs, small bones, dried peas, and peach stones, each standing for a numerical value. Before the counting starts, all the counters are heaped in one corner. The person doing the calculation then moves them about while chanting certain rules learned by rote. The machine can do anything from addition to division, and it can even be used to calculate up to eighteen digits, according to some claims.

Three times a year, the four finance officers submit to the Dalai Lama or the regent through the cabinet a list of qualified students for government service. Once approved, the candidate curls his hair into two knots on the crown of his head. These are an unmistakable sign of a Tibetan nobleman who has joined government service.

From the date a candidate is enrolled in either the ecclesiastical or the secular training school, he is already considered to be in government service. He will be assigned a position in all the public functions, in keeping with his rank and seniority. After graduation, he becomes a probationary officer, awaiting an appointment.

The Tse-Drung, because of their training under the secretariat, are supposed to be better versed in literature; while the Ku-Dra, because of their training in the finance school, are considered more adept in arithmetic. Literature and arithmetic are considered the two fundamentals for a public servant. To become a public servant is to become a *Pon-Po*, a term which the Tibetans use to address members of the ruling class. A commoner may work for the government, of course, but there is no career for him there. He can at most be a high clerk, never crossing the line into Pon-Po status.

The four cabinet ministers, the four grand secretaries, and the four finance officers are the twelve persons who run the political show of Tibet. There are many other offices under the cabinet headed by chiefs of a higher official rank than the grand secretaries and the finance officers, but only these twelve persons really count in both formulating policies and laws and seeing to justice and general administration. Metaphorically, the Tibetans refer to the cabinet ministers as the "Four External Pillars" and to the grand secretaries and finance officers as the "Eight Internal Pillars" which sustain the structure of the Tibetan government.

## The Administration

To measure the Tibetan government by a strictly modern yardstick would be a waste of time. Every governing entity, from the state to the feudal lord or the monastery, is a complete government in itself. We have said something already about the Tibetan legislature as a mere instrument of the executive branch. Nearly the same statement might be made about the judiciary. We know of only one office in the whole of Tibet which deals with capital crimes. There is no court, as such; every government office and indeed all officers in both the ecclesiastical and secular courts may sit as court of law. Tibetans are notorious litigants, however, and few peoples in the world are such eloquent pleaders. Appeals may be addressed to any office to which the disputants belong, or even directly to the Dalai Lama or his regent. Thus, from the cabinet on down, the whole government thrusts a finger into the judicial pie. One hears often of a case being dragged on for months or years and fortunes being spent by both disputants before the case dies a natural death. One standing practice is the appointment by the cabinet ministers of special committees for hearing important cases. This appointment is a favor only to be gained at a high price.

Two famous legal codes exist in Tibet, one allegedly produced by no less a celebrity than the seventh century king Son-Tsan Gam-Po, and the other by the brilliant Gyan-Ch'u Gye-Tshen of the Pha-Mo-Dru-Pa family in the fourteenth century. The first of these codes, whose authorship is open to dispute, consists of ten commandments for the holy order, and sixteen articles for the laity. They are still regarded as the basic moral code for every Tibetan today. The group of thirteen commandments by Gyan-Ch'u Gye-Tshen is much more elaborate and covers everything from petty thefts to the conduct of a ruler. It is the most comprehensive and authoritative code of Tibet. It advocates, among other things, trial by ordeal after oath taking before a god.

The whole government is thus comprised of nothing but the executive arm. But before describing that arm, we want to point out a few relevant facts. First of all, Tibetans attach an overwhelming importance to the status of a government official or Pon-Po. A nobleman who is not a Pon-Po has almost no public status. And once a Pon-Po, he becomes a different man, even to his own wife and children. His dress, the number of his attendants, the trappings of his horse together with the height and quality of his seat— everything is prescribed for him, and any deviation will bring him official censure.

Second, despite the fuss the Tibetans make about rank and position, there seems to be little systematization yet in their official grading. Among the secular officers, only those of the fourth rank are currently known by their title, Rim-Zhi, while the titles for ranks above and below this are understood. The clerical officers are named according to their posts. Little if any change has been made in this regard since the reforms of Emperor Chien Lung, at the end of the eighteenth century. Third, there seems to be no fixed scale of pay, increase, or advancement for the government servants. Except for a few high posts like the ministerships, to which a government estate is attached whose yields go to the incumbent as part of his payment, the general salary scale is so ridiculously low that it would be deemed inadequate even for servants. Theoretically, of course, since every clerical and lay official is already invested with regular endowments, he should not get further pay for services which he is bound by duty to render. A monk officer is supposed to live on his monastic alms collections and government subsidies; a lay officer, who is always of the nobility, can subsist on the income from his family estate. But since such emoluments are never enough to meet the demands of a public official, how the system works out in actual practice is not difficult to see.

Below the cabinet, and in addition to the secretariat and finance office, there are a number of old and new offices, staffed equally by clerical and lay officials. Among the older offices are two important stewardships which are general caterers respectively to the Dalai Lama with his court and to the cabinet with its many subordinate offices at Lhasa. Among the new offices, most of which were created by a Chinese Amban over forty years ago, are those of industry, agriculture, and tea and salt taxation, along with a foreign office, which is a still later addition. These offices are headed by a class of senior officials ranking directly below the cabinet ministers. Though in point of rank they are above the grand secretaries and the finance officers, who are all in the fourth rank, yet they play no vital role in Tibetan politics, being mostly elder statesmen looking for sinecures or retirement. Whenever a ministership is vacant, it is always the grand secretaries and the finance officers who get a promotion over and above the heads of these elder statesmen.

No such division of functions as is mentioned above characterizes the local administrations of Tibet, whether large or small. These are all miniature governments. There are roughly three classes of local governments in Tibet: the village under a headman, the magistracy under a magistrate, and the regional government under a governor. Several villages make a magistracy, or Dsong (Fort), which in former times was always the site where a fort commander, Dsong-Pon, had his headquarters. Since the unification of Tibet under the lamaist regime, however, the Dsong-Pon has become more and more a civil officer, the magistrate of today. But even now, the office of a Dsong is always in one of the old but strong fortresses, crowning the tops of craggy hills, which stand guard over the Tibetan valleys. The Dsong fortresses bring vividly to mind earlier times when enemy raids were frequent in this country. It was from such a fortress that the proud Potala at Lhasa grew since its founding almost thirteen hundred years ago.

A Dsong-Pon, though a most awesome figure in his magistracy, is always only a junior clerical or lay officer. He is always an absentee, living in luxury at Lhasa, while the magistracy is left to his private secretary or steward. The idea of private ownership is so strongly entrenched in the Tibetan mind that he who gets appointed to a Dsong, or for that matter to any government post, regards it as something he has leased from which he is free to make as much as possible before he quits.

Besides Lhasa and its suburbs, which are under the charge of two local administrations, there are in Tibet about eight regional governments, each under a governor, most commonly called Chi-Ch'ub. The most important of these governors is the one stationed at Chamdo, in Kham. According to the present custom, this governor, who is in charge of a vast territory from the west bank of the Kinsha-kiang to the eastern border of the region Kong-Po, is of ministerial rank. His authority is said to be next after that of the cabinet.

Another important office is that of the northern governor, located at Nag-Ch'u-Kha, astride the ancient communication lines between Koko Nor and

Lhasa. Two governors are posted there, one monk officer and one lay, both of the fourth rank. Similarly, there is a southern governor near Tse-Thang, situated at the mouth of the Yar-Lung valley. Only one governor resides there, a clerical officer of the fourth rank. There are also governors of the fourth rank at Shigatse, the capital of Tsang, and at Dro-Mo and Ding-Ri, which guard the routes to India and Nepal. The governor of Nga-Ri in western Tibet may also be mentioned in this category, since his post was raised to the fourth rank a few years back.

Tibet has a fighting force of a sort. The recruitment of the Tibetan soldier is, like all services, done on the basis of Khrai. In charge of the recruitment is the office of the commanders in chief. It is curious that even the war office is manned by a mixed clerical and lay staff on the principal of equal representation, under the joint charge of two commanders in chief, one clerical and one secular. The army itself, however, has been kept clear of clerical participation. It is organized on the basic unit of five hundred men. There were said to be twelve or thirteen of these units in the standing army before its clash with the Chinese People's Liberation Army in 1950. Each such unit is named after a letter of the Tibetan alphabet and is placed under a commander. Under him are two assistant commanders, each in charge of two hundred fifty men. To become a military officer of the rank of commander or assistant commander, no qualification is required except that the candidate be of the nobility. Nor is any training required after the appointment. In other words, any noble in civil service can some day transfer to a military post, and vice versa. Only lower ranks are open to the common soldiers. There is, therefore, very little comradeship between the high command and the soldiers.

The Tibetan army, with its complete lack of modern equipment and poor leadership, is not taken seriously even by Tibetans themselves. The monks detest it as an imported hybrid. The nobility distrusts it as a potential menace. And the common people fear it as a public scourge. Yet no one can question the Tibetan soldier's individual bravery, his great capacity for standing hardship and privation, his loyalty, his physical stamina, and the many other qualities which make a fine soldier. Once he is trained in modern weapons, properly organized and led, there can be no doubt that he will turn out to be a most formidable fighter, especially on the mountainous tracts and high terrain of Tibet.

# part five

## Life with the Tibetan People

### Inhabitants of the Promised Wonderland

The moment you set foot in Tibet, the first question to cross your mind is: "Is this Shangri-La, the promised wonderland?" Tibet at first sight looks hardly different from the surrounding countries; it is only more bleak and barren and wrapped in a deeper sort of silence.

As you penetrate farther into this country, jogging along at a caravan pace, the monotony and desolation of the landscape begin to stir you with strange thoughts and fancies, between moments of mental torpor. The mountains, the valleys, and the lakes are grander and mightier than anything you are used to; the expansive sky, the crystal atmosphere, from which sudden hailstorms and blizzards are unleashed with brutal force, look formidable. And the immensity of the silence is at times overwhelming.

The first Tibetan you come across is inevitably a muleteer. Dressed in a voluminous grayish coarse woolen gown tucked up knee-high and dark thick woolen boots, he is all good humor and obsequiousness. From under the brim of his weather-beaten hat, he peers at you with genuine or simulated fear and puts out his tongue in deference every time his eyes meet yours. A metal ring about three inches in diameter dangles below his left ear, and the thin, threadbare lash of a whip protrudes sideways from his waistband. He stalks patiently behind his mule trains, whose leaders are garlanded with red tassels and resonant bells that boom on the silence a good distance ahead. Occasionally he gets excited at a straying mule and shouts and scolds, cracking his whip or throwing stones with marvelous marksmanship. Otherwise he takes it easy, mumbling the Tibetan prayer *Om Ma Ni Pa Me Hum* while darning the sole of a boot or spinning with a dangling spindle. All day he is on the move, sallying here and there to gather droppings from passing cattle.

A half-brother to the muleteer is the shepherd, to be met on the slopes, beside running brooks, or wherever there are small patches of green to give a treat to the eyes. While the flocks are grazing, he squats on the ground with his family before a black yak-hair fabric tent, preparing his tea and barley meal. He throws two or three handfuls of sheep dung or a few cakes of yak dung between two stones, strikes up a fire, and fans it with a roundish bellows made of sheepskin. A little blue smoke curls up from the teapot, spreading a sense of homeliness in the wild. The family pass around a Tsam-Pa bag, from which they pour out a portion of the barley meal into the wooden bowls they carry, and begin their meal in silence.

To such a wayside party sometimes comes a weary pilgrim. Perhaps he hails from the border of Szechuan or Kansu and is on a three-year tour to the holy places of Tibet to fulfill a vow. He carries on his back all his worldly belongings in a tiny bundle. In one hand he holds a long stick with a pointed metal head and in the other a prayer wheel. He joins in the party like an expected friend, swapping tales with them about their rambles. Perhaps he asks whether anybody happened to notice two women passing there a few months ago on their way farther west. They were his relatives. He was put on their trail by a lama at the hermitage twenty days' journey to the northeast. After some recollection, one of the party recalls that he certainly saw a young woman and an old one, but they were accompanied by a trader from Kham. Which way did they go? To the west. The pilgrim bids them goodbye and sets his face to the west.

Every water divide is a *La* in Tibet, and every La is marked with heaps of stones, called *Do-Pung*. On reaching a divide, the traveler doffs his hat and, after a silent prayer to the spirit of the mountain, throws a stone on the cairn as an offering. Overhanging the cairns, tied to a cord between two poles, are five-colored prayer flags, called *Dar-Cho*. The flags are filled with miniature prints of the prayer *Om Ma Ni Pa Me Hum*, which are thus continuously wafted heavenward by the mountain breeze. The traveler now gives a lusty piercing yell, as only a mountaineer can do, to celebrate his conquest of the heights, and listens to the sound echoing and re-echoing over the mountaintops. Then, as his parting offering, he ties a piece of old cloth on the flagpole,

*Life with the Tibetan People*

leaving it there on the windy heights. Tibet is a poor country and he is a poor traveler.

The approach to a village or monastery is marked by a *Mani* wall* or by a pagoda. The wall is about as tall as a man and from forty to two hundred feet in length. It is mostly plastered with yellow clay, a sign of holiness, and along its upper part are votive stones, mostly slabs of granite, carved with images of gods, goddesses, or mantras in bold coloring. The pagoda is an architectural symbol of the four basic elements which, according to Buddhist theory, make up our world. The part of the pagoda at ground level, sometimes with doors and sometimes without, symbolizes the earth; the middle portion, in which religious relics are deposited, stands for water; the cylindrical neck is fire; and the top, in the form of a sun inside a crescent, represents ether and air. Both the groundwork and the middle portion are whitewashed, while the upper parts are painted in gold.

At the foot of such a wall or pagoda are sometimes seated old men and women turning prayer wheels, counting beads, and muttering holy verses all at one time. They are devoting their twilight days to accumulating merits for the next life and, incidentally, to collecting a few extra alms.

A small cluster of stone huts boasts the name of a village. The huts are only stone and mortar versions of the tents. Looking inside, you will see nothing but a few cooking utensils, a water pitcher, a plow, and a spade. You now meet the cultivator of the land. He shares the home with the animals he keeps. A rich family may have a few cushions on wooden frames and a table like a footstool. The very rich have an altar behind a row of copper cups filled with plain water. The inmates—men, women, and children—look dirty, especially the women, whose faces are smeared with catechu. Some say this is to protect their complexions, but others think it is to prevent them from seducing the monks.

These women, with blackened faces, goggling eyes, and white teeth, are always busy. They work at the loom, or they are busy making tea or churning milk in a tub. They sing as they work. They fetch water in a wooden pitcher, which they carry on their backs, or they help their mates at the plow in the field. Wherever they go, they bring along their tiny chubby children, many of whom are partially or entirely nude no matter how cold the weather.

It is perhaps plowingtime. A pair of sturdy hairy Dzo, a crossbreed of yaks and oxen, is festooned with red and white tufts from horn to horn. The men shout and halloo, and the beasts grunt and stumble, scratching the bare surface of the unyielding ground. Occasionally the blast of a deep throbbing trumpet stirs the still air. Then, later, the faint whining melody of a pair of

* A wall on which the prayer *Om Ma Ni Pa Me Hum* is inscribed.

　　　　　　　　　　　　　　　　　　　*Tibet and the Tibetans*

clarinets fills the evening with haunting and melancholy music. It comes from the lonely lofty monastery on some inaccessible height, which appears to the wayfarer like the white speck of a bird's nest. The lamas are beginning their evening prayer.

The plowman goes home. A noisy caravan arrives amid the barking of leonine Tibetan dogs. The muleteers scurry around, unloading the leather-bound packages and feeding themselves and their animals. The boys herd the sheep home and tie them by the feet in long lines neck to neck, while chattering women come with buckets to milk them. The weary traveler hunts for a night's lodging, for which he offers a quarter brick of Szechuanese tea. Life bustles before the last flicker of the setting sun. Visits are paid, news is exchanged, and small bargains are made. As soon as the cold silent night spreads over the country, all mumble their last prayers. Then men, women, children, and strangers curl up within their voluminous clothes, in one heap, as they do from the upper steppes of Mongolia to the windy plateau of Tibet. Thus they sleep in peace under the serene and protecting gaze of their savior, Lord Buddha.

## Tibetan Etiquette

When you draw near the heart of the hermit kingdom, you begin to experience moments of difficult mental adjustment. You realize that you are heading into a society fossilized many centuries back, and that you are supposed to behave there like one of its members. It will not be like your first meeting with the rustics, for rustics are the same everywhere; a pastoral charm clings to them. And with the rustics you are merely a spectator. But now, as you approach the center of Tibetan civilization, everything hardens in the mold of a harsh tradition that dictates what you must do and what you must not, and turns all your social contacts into dry dead formalities.

You get a foretaste of what is coming when you meet the headman. He is a typical country squire. Cleaner and better groomed than the villagers, he comes to you with three or four servants bearing armfuls of gifts. Since you are traveling by government corvée, as everybody of any consequence does in Tibet, he is the man you have your first dealings with. He wears a dark full-length gown with long sleeves, a red waistband, a long earring, and a long queue ending in a red tassel. On seeing you, he shuffles into position to present to you, with both hands, a flowing white silk scarf, *Kha-Ja*, the first item required in Tibetan social intercourse. His other presents are then displayed before you: the dried carcass of a sheep, a bag of fodder, butter, and a basket of eggs, of which—as is no longer a secret—probably ninety percent are rotten. Then, bending with his saucer hat in hand, he mumbles something between gasps to the effect that he has brought your honor a few humble things from his poor country and hopes your honor will not disdain them. Your honor's living quarters have been cleared and made clean; water, fuel, fodder, and servants have been provided. Your honor must not hesitate to command him in case anything should be wanting, at it is his duty to see to your honor's comfort during your honor's stay. Whatever you say, he affirms by catching his breath, scratching his ear, and uttering a monosyllable, *Lo*. For anything he cannot provide, his excuses are abundant. Then backing away from your presence, he draws up to the full height of a headman and issues orders left and right, as befits his position. However, the next moment he sights you, he cowers like a beaten dog, and pulling out his tongue, peers at you from the corner of his eyes. Tomorrow he will come to collect his dues on his goods, services, and civility.

The silk scarf, or Kha-Ta, he presents to you comes from Chengtu, Szechuan. An absolute necessity for all social occasions, it is, generally speaking, one of three kinds. The best of these scarves is of pure silk, about twelve feet long by three feet wide, bordered with swastika patterns and sometimes with Buddha's image woven in the center. Such a Kha-Ta is to be presented only to the Dalai Lama, Panchen Lama, and the highest incarnation lamas. The second kind of Kha-Ta, which is also made of silk with swastika borders, is about nine feet long and three feet wide. It is used among the upper classes. The third kind, which is of mixed silk and flax and is much smaller, is meant for the lower classes. Just as there are three kinds of Kha-Ta, there are also three ways of presenting it. To one who is your superior, you should raise it in both hands to the height of your forehead. To an equal, you are to offer it on a level with your shoulders and take one in return from him. To one who is below you, you should spread it on his nape.

The language the headman speaks is also different from that the country folks use. He speaks *Zhe-Sa*, the honorific language. In its finer shades, the Tibetan language is capable of three distinctions: the most honorific, the less honorific, and the nonhonorific, to be applied respectively to your superiors, your equals, and your inferiors. For general purposes, the distinction between the honorific and the nonhonorific is essential. It is not merely a matter of a few expressions but involves two sets of vocabulary. Nouns, pronouns, adjectives, verbs, and adverbs are all governed by the law. Thus, among the polished society everything gets an honorific and a nonhonorific name—everything, that is, except the sun, the moon, heaven, and hell, which cannot be associated with private ownership. Otherwise, there is a Zhe-Sa term for every word from your hair to your foot, and from the hat and shoes you wear to the horses and dogs you keep. And to muddle up the terms for your puppies with those of your friend's puppies would be a faux pas in common courtesy.

Your headman is the epitome of Tibetan etiquette. This etiquette demands not only that he should cower before you with proper humility because you are above him but also that he should exercise proper authority over all who are below him. The rule is to let everyone behave according to his status. Just as an inferior should behave as an inferior, a superior will not be exempted from censure if he does not behave like a superior. If you know some rudiments of the rule, the moment you come into contact with a Tibetan you will be able to tell from his manner, address, and language in which stratum of society he proposes to assign you a place.

When you get to Lhasa you will see class distinction carried to perfection. You can, for instance, tell the rank of every officer in the street at a glance. Junior officers from the sixth rank and below wear dark woolen gowns and have one servant. Their horses have one small red tassel in front. The fourth-rank officers wear yellow silk gowns, ride horses with two tassels, and are accompanied by two servants. The senior officers above fourth rank wear brownish-yellow silk gowns with large dragon patterns. And the cabinet ministers wear light yellow silk gowns with circular patterns of dragons, and keep six servants, plus one junior officer as their herald. To become a minister is to reach the acme of honor. Each time a minister mounts and dismounts, the herald bows low toward him; and when he goes about, the herald clears the way for him with a whip. Riders are to climb down and salute. Pedestrians should stand aside, with their hats in their hands and their tongues hanging out. A minister is euphuistically referred to as *Zhab-Pe* (the Lotus Seat of Buddha) and addressed as *Sa-Wang-Ch'en-Po* (the Great Power on Earth). When he stands up, everyone must stand up, and no one must sit down before he is seated. His chair is five feet high. His cushion must be of fine brocade with certain colors and designs, and even the stuffing is made to order. The cup he drinks from is cylindrical; and in certain public functions tea is served him by his herald kneeling on one knee.

This class distinction in every detail of daily life comes so much as a matter of course to the Tibetan ruling class that any slight departure from its rules jars on their nerves if it does not break their hearts. They ask how public order is to be maintained once such distinctions are removed. They can never understand how the President of the United States is to be distinguished from other citizens if he is dressed like any American businessman. The Tibetans know only one form of courtesy and that is their own brand.

*Life with the Tibetan People*                                                            121

In the Tibetan vocabulary they have no honorific word yet for "democracy." In fact, they openly scorn it. Wherever confusion reigns, some wit is sure to say, "What's on—democracy?"

## An Audience with the Dalai Lama

No one at his arrival in Lhasa is to make any official call on anybody before he pays his respects to the Dalai Lama. It is a rule, and any departure from it is the height of imprudence.

In embarking on any worth-while project in Tibet, the first thing to do is to pick an auspicious date. If you are paying your first visit to the Dalai, the date is of course not to be fixed by you but by the office *Tse-Ga*, the "Front of the Peak." The presentation often takes place at the morning audience of the Dalai with his clerical court. There are other important occasions when outsiders are received, notably those ceremonies on the days of the Dalai Lama's removal to his summer palace, Nor-Bu Ling-Ka, and his return to his winter quarters at the Potala. Another such occasion is the Tibetan New Year. The most elaborate audience occurs on New Year's Day, when, after paying your respects to His Holiness, you sit out the whole function which follows. No personal intercourse between the Dalai Lama and you is to be contemplated. There is not even a chance of hearing his voice except perhaps on one or two occasions such as we experienced with the present Dalai. This honor is not to be passed over in silence.

We have attended many such functions, and we propose to describe the New Year audience, such as we know it, by way of illustration. It takes place early in the morning, indeed so inconveniently early in the biting cold of the Lhasa winter that we have to rise long before the break of day in order to attend on His Holiness in time. The hall in the uppermost story of the Potala in which the function takes place is about ninety feet long and sixty feet wide with a skylight in the middle. Occupying the upper end is a spacious dais five feet high, on which stands the equally high gilt throne of the Dalai. Right above the dais is suspended a rescript board in Emperor Chien Lung's own handwriting—four Chinese characters with Manchurian, Mongolian, and Tibetan translations, extolling the pacification of the remote territories. The throne of the Dalai always faces south. A few steps to the right and facing in the same direction is a raised seat for the preceptor.

Only these two seats face the south, the rest being arranged along the other three sides of the hall. Most conspicuous of all are the high seats for the regent and the prime minister at right angles to the Dalai's throne and to the right of it. Behind these seats are places for the high incarnation lamas of the Three Seats of Learning, who squat on cushions on the floor, each cushion varying in thickness according to the status of the occupant.

Farther down, separated by a passage from the entrance, are rows of carpets for the high executives of the three monasteries. Occupying the foremost seats in the first row are the two alternate candidates for the Ge-Lu papacy (Gan-Dan Khri-Pa himself being, as a rule, absent), and below them all the abbots of the three monasteries in the order of seniority. The lesser dignitaries are ranged behind them.

At right angles to the rows of lama dignitaries—that is, opposite the Dalai's throne—are thin cushions for the higher-ranking officers of the secular court. The first row is occupied by the four cabinet ministers and the senior officers above the fourth rank, while the rows behind are for the fourth rankers and sons of especially illustrious families. Small footstool-like tables, varying in height and size, are provided for the first row. The same detailed gradation in the thickness of the cushions, their quality, color, and pattern applies to all the seats.

Opposite the lama dignitaries—that is, at the left of the dais—are the lower-ranking officers, from the fifth rank and below. The first row, however, is reserved for the representatives of the Chinese Central government. On both flanks of the dais along the walls are more seats for the high clerical officers, such as the grand secretaries. Since the ceremony takes place within the empty square in front of the dais, the presence of these officers is not often noticeable.

When we are all assembled in the hall, the deep voice of a herald announces the approach of the Dalai Lama. Next, the music of two clarinets is heard. Then a monk officer appears at the entrance and hurriedly unrolls a long strip of yellow carpet reaching to the foot of the dais, while another, bearing a big bundle of yellow silk on top of his head, walks in and spreads it on the throne. Other monk officers follow with cups and trays all covered with brocade. Two more attendants arrive with charcoal burners, in which they put sandalwood to perfume the room. Then come two bearers of incense burners, two clarinet players, the prime minister with the four cabinet ministers, four giant guards, four abbots of the Rear, the regent, and the Dalai Lama amid a host of lesser clerical followers. All stand up and bow till the Dalai is seated on his throne.

The music stops. The Tibetan officials, from the regent on down, standing in disarray before the dais, fold their hands above their heads and go down on their knees, touching their foreheads to the ground three times. There seems to be no attempt at a concerted movement. A long single file is formed, led to the throne by the ministers and senior officers. Each presents a Kha-Ta to the Dalai and, turning left, gives another to the regent. In return, the Dalai and the regent place their hands once on the head of each, as a lama blessing. All this is done under the vigilance of the giant guards, who constantly remind everyone not to hold up the line. If you are a man of some consequence, your turn will come after the fourth rankers and the sons of the top-class nobility. Before presenting your Kha-Ta to the Dalai, you are required to perform the act of four offerings, an act of extreme humility, before the living Buddha. The first offering may be a sort of fancy cake on a plate, with flowing ribbons of five colors, which you must put on your shoulder. This signifies your wholehearted dedication. The second is a small Buddha image, which represents Buddha's body. The third, a volume of holy scripture, represents Buddha's words. The fourth is a tiny pagoda, symbolic of Buddha's mind. The same process is repeated before the regent, though the four symbols are of a smaller size.

Lower-ranking officials and some of the Dalai's court attendants are at the rear of the queue. Both the Dalai and the regent take up a baton with a colored tassel like a mosquito whisk at one end, and instead of using their hands they bless these late-comers with a touch of the whisk on their heads.

While the procession is in progress, your attention is aroused by a piercing yell. Two abbots selected from among the members of the three principal monasteries, nearly stripped to the waist, advance to the upper end of the hall. They are starting a religious disputation. They debate with many poses and gestures. The theme and the language are so profound that only a few lamas can understand them. At one point, we are told, the theme is the demarcation between the past, the present, and the future; at another, it is the identity of the self in dreams with the self after death.

When all are seated, the grand steward comes around to convey the Dalai's greetings to everybody, and all stand up to give their thanks. Then the steward conducts two monk officials into the court, the Dalai's chef and his assistant, the latter holding on his shoulder a pot of tea wrapped in brocade. They march to the front of the dais, and one attendant abbot comes down to receive the pot. The chef produces his own wooden cup, into which the abbot pours a few drops of the tea. Then, kneeling on one knee before the throne, the chef drains the cup to demonstrate that it is not poisoned. He waits until the pot is given back; then he is led with his assistant out of the court.

The disputation stops at a signal from the grand steward after the Dalai's first tea. Amid lively music of drums and fifes full of exotic charm, thirteen silk-clad boy dancers troop into the hall, each with a wooden ax, and start a dance characterized by jerky angular movements which remind you of the figures in Indian paintings and sculpture. The dance is called *Gar* and is said to have been imported from Ladakh by the fifth Dalai Lama. When the dance is over, the dancers back out, single file, bowing low to the throne.

The disputation starts once more, and the second tea is served to the Dalai Lama in the same manner as the first. The rule is to serve tea thrice while the disputation is in progress, and the Gar dance comes after each tea. The function ends with the last dance. At another word from the deep organ voice of the giant guard, the whole court scrambles to its feet and bows till the Dalai retires with his suite, amid clarinet music.

But we must not omit an interlude which supplies a sort of climax to the whole show. During the intermission between the first and second teas, servants bring in heaps of Tibetan delicacies, which are displayed before the dais. The edibles include dried almonds and other nuts, dried carcasses of sheep, and pyramids of fried cakes. These are the Dalai's New Year gifts to be distributed to all present. However, when about one-third are left, at a certain signal, a score of servants rush from nowhere toward the gifts, and a free-for-all ensues. Each grabs as much as he can, stuffing it into his dress, and some come equipped with a huge gunnysack. A few minutes are allowed for the pandemonium; then the giant guards close in. While the guards' whips swish and crack over shoulders and backs, the poor people continue to scramble and scrape for every fragment till nothing is left. These delicacies, being fresh from the kitchen of the Dalai Lama, are deemed efficacious in curing diseases. On about half a dozen occasions each year, these poor servants are allowed a share of the delicacies at the price of a few blows. The spoils thus earned are sold, and fetch good money.

It is amazing to see how fervently the average Tibetan feels toward his religious head and how his attachment is at times rewarded. We remember one occasion when the Dalai Lama paid a rare visit to Lhasa and held his court in the Central Cathedral. A huge crowd gathered below where he was staying, hoping to get a glimpse of him. This spontaneous flow of loyalty, which elsewhere would probably have called forth appropriate acknowledgment, met with an unexpected reception here. The giant guards sallied forth into the crowd and dealt blows with their whips left and right, such blows as might have been given to the most undeserving. Our Tibetan friends assured us that the masses did not resent such treatment. No, they do not yet. But once they do, what is there to stop their resentment?

## Tibetan Hospitality

Tibetans, perhaps still adhering to the code of the nomads, are noted for their hospitality. Giving parties is among both high and low a popular recreation. The parties given by the nobles may last from ten to fifteen days. Hundreds of guests are invited by turns, and many stay overnight. Toward the end scarcely a host fails to provide more fun for his closest circle of friends for another couple of days and nights.

If you are not on intimate terms with the host, you are not likely to find his party a very lively affair. The invitation is usually oral. The host's butler comes with a Kha-Ta and discharges his mission in an ornate speech which leaves the time unspecified. The ambiguity does no harm, however. On the appointed day it is the custom of a good host to send his servant three times to hasten your arrival. The first summons comes early in the morning, and the second not much later. The third arrives near midday. And, as all who have experienced it know, this is the time when a respectable guest prepares to go. An unfortunate friend of ours who answered the first summons was embarrassed to rouse his host from his bed.

Respectable houses in Tibet are built of solid stone. While commoners live in one-story or two-story buildings, the house of a noble in a place like Lhasa is always a three-story one, shut in with high thick walls like a castle. The walls, some of them four to five feet thick, taper slightly toward the top. The house, which is whitewashed and has dark-framed windows, bears a modern look that belies its interior. A Tibetan house is dark, ill-paved, ill-ventilated, and ill-planned, and about three-fifths is wasted space.

When you ride to a *Zim-Sha*, as the house of a noble is honorifically known, you see a wooden gate in a painted frame, flanked by two low stone platforms. We have taken it for granted that you are riding, because nobody of consequence ever walks in Tibet, least of all to attend a party. You use the two platforms for mounting and dismounting, providing that you are socially inferior to your host.

On entering the gate, you find yourself in a square stone-paved courtyard before the main building. Around three sides runs a two-story gallery, the ground floor of which is used as a stable. The upper floor is a long, sheltered corridor opening into the kitchen or servants' quarters.

The entry to the main building is like the first gate, complete with two stone platforms for the more honored guests. Somewhere around the corners are chained the ferocious Tibetan mastiffs, which snarl and roar at every stranger. These giant woolly beasts with bloodshot eyes are chained all their lives, which obviously maddens their tempers.

Unless you are an exceptionally high personage, your host is not likely to meet you at the door. His steward or relative will welcome you here. You are now ushered into a gloomy entrance, where the first thing to attract your attention is a mural of a Mongolian hero tackling a tiger. Some say he is Ku-Shi Khan, the Mongolian prince who put the Fifth Dalai Lama on the lamaist throne; others consider the figures of religious significance; but all believe the picture to be an effective talisman in keeping off undesirable elements. A mural of this kind guards the entrance to every noble house in Lhasa.

A dark slippery staircase leads up to the second floor. It is cleaner and better lit than the ground floor because it is built around the central open courtyard. The house of every well-to-do Tibetan has at least one family chapel, and a nobleman's house has two. The larger chapel usually occupies the central front portion of this floor. It is dark and moldy, with dusty images and bookshelves which remind you of a lamasery. The room is only occasionally used, as for the New Year, marriages, and official promotions. The rest of the floor is abandoned to servants, poor relations, and general storage.

All comfort and luxury are centered on the top floor, where the family quarters are. Accordingly, you will find your host welcoming you at the head of the second staircase. The top floor generally covers only the back part of the house, the front portion being uncovered and forming a sort of roof garden. Consequently, every room faces south, sunlight being a necessity with these highland people. Many of these rooms have glass windows and doors, which open to a roof of Tibetan cement.

The best room on the whole floor, hence of the whole house, is the second family chapel. It is also your host's study-sitting room, if not also his bedroom. Here he spends the greatest part of his time. It is draped with colored silks and brocades and covered with carpets. Gilt images on gilt altars peep out from behind shining copper cups, butter lamps, flour offerings, fine bronze, rare porcelain, and curios. A few cheap tawdry things also find their way to the altars—such things as a glass ball, a baby's toy fan, or an empty bottle of modern perfume. Along the walls are hung painted scrolls on rich brocade mountings, called *Thang-Ka*, depicting stories from the Buddhist pantheon. Below the scrolls are gilt or fancy-colored cabinets. Embroidered silk draperies fill up more space, and the walls themselves are painted over with pictures and auspicious designs, as are the beams and pillars also. One chief drawback with Tibetan houses is that, because of the lack of good long timber, the interior is full of pillars. It is a custom to measure the size of a room by counting the number of pillars in it. On festive occasions, the pillars, too, are covered with scarlet velvet. Wooden floors are not yet popular. But whether made of wood or cement, the floors are carefully polished with butter. Tibetan ceilings, latticeworks of twigs and beams from which dust and stones fall at the least provocation, are another drawback. A silk cloth is always suspended below them. Wooden ceilings are coming into fashion, however, as are chairs and sofas. As all Tibetans sit cross-legged, Buddha-fashion, a common arrangement is to put thick cushions around a pair of rectangular tables which form a square. The tables are finely lacquered, and the cushions are covered with fancy carpets. The height of the cushion is in direct proportion to your status. But as the height of the table does not change, the higher your climb the more unbearable is your position when you have to bend down to the table, which is often on a level with the seat.

Tibetan etiquette uses a strict yardstick. The host goes to the front gate to wait on an exceptionally honored guest; for those less exceptionally honored, he waits at the second door; for other honored guests, he comes to the staircase; for those who are slightly below him, he goes to the door of his reception room; and as for those who are decidedly below him, they will have to come to him instead. The rule also applies at the time of departure. At big parties, only the most honored guests are invited to stay with the host, while guests of lesser importance are assigned to their proper rooms. And, at all orthodox Tibetan parties, ladies and gentlemen are kept in separate compartments.

The first item on the menu is Tibetan tea. It is served in beautiful china or jade cups with silver or gold covers and stands. A servant, stationed near by with a shining pot, comes to pour more into your cup after each sip. Though Tibetan tea tastes like soup, it is still preferable to the Chinese tea Tibetans serve, according to our experience. With tea conversation begins, amid compliments and talk of the weather. Tibetans are famous for their reserve, and they are even more remarkable for their ability to keep countenance. They delight in pretending ignorance, though quite often their ignorance is genuine. They like to pound you with questions, professing to admire your judgment and profundity while secretly forming their own opinions. When supernatural matters are touched on, then they give inexhaustible accounts of the miracles and marvels in which Tibet abounds.

A fashionable party in Lhasa comprises a light midday meal, a lavish dinner, and a tea in between. Except for the afternoon tea, which is Western-style, all food is cooked and served Chinese fashion. A twelve- to fifteen-course dinner is a common occurrence. Wine drinking is a great art, and the host will resort to any means, fair or foul, to persuade his guests to drink more. Finger guessing is a popular game. Noise is enjoyed for its own sake. To give the proper atmosphere, the host often hires "wine maids," some professional, who come in a Tibetan lady's gala dress resplendent in jewels and ornaments.

They bear in huge jugs of Tibetan wine, called *Ch'ang*, a brew made from barley and tasting like beer. They smile and smirk, and with their sweet persuasiveness and dazzling presence they radiate charm and mirth all around and seldom fail to refill a cup.

To amuse guests in the long afternoon, the host provides plenty of indoor games—dice throwing, dominoes, Tibetan cards, and mah-jongg. There are also opera singers seated outside, who are kept in high spirits with Ch'ang. Once they start a chorus, all conversation stops. A tamer affair is a Tibetan dance. An orchestra of five or six musicians with Chinese instruments furnishes the background for two or three women dancers. The dancers line up on a wooden plank and stamp to the rhythm of the music and sing in an impossible falsetto. Much grace characterizes the older tunes, while the new ones are lively and brisk. All the charm of the dance lies in the foot movement, the upper part of the body being kept steady. Occasionally, men join in, and then the dance becomes quick and strenuous.

With dinner comes the excitement of wine dueling. But the greatest excitement of a Tibetan party comes in its breaking up. It occurs at the most awkward moment, when your head is reeling and your legs are benumbed from squatting through the long feast. Every eye is on the number one guest of honor. As soon as he moves, everyone rushes for the door. As most parties last well after dark, the rooms are lit by a few gas lamps. But these lamps move like planets round the guest of honor, and the moment he leaves, most of the lights leave with him. It is then you discover how defective an otherwise perfect-looking Tibetan house is. The doors are low. Thresholds are high. You stumble. You knock your head. The stairs are precipitous and too narrow for a foothold. You slip. Down in the courtyard, horses neigh and rear with fright at the glaring lights, dogs bark, masters shout for servants, and servants search for masters. Good-byes are hastily exchanged in the dark. Horses start bucking and whirling to move, as stragglers are in the way and servants are swarming about. Then at last there is a clatter of hoofs, and everybody is outside the gate. Whew, it is like a battlefield!

We never understand why there should be so much haste in leaving a Tibetan party. But the mood seems catching. As to what happens to those left behind, we never know.

# How Tibetans Live

There are three main groups of people in Tibet: the nomads, the farmers, and the townsfolk.

The life of the nomads is much the same as in the days of the king Son-Tsan Gam-Po in the seventh century. Clad in bulky, raw sheepskins, they roam about the northern plateau of Tibet with their flocks, and many die without seeing what a Tibetan village is like. They have a bronze complexion, a sturdy figure, and a noble bearing that reminds many travelers of American Indians. Their women plait their hair into many tiny queues, which are then bundled into a big one below the nape and adorned artistically with red and yellow stones. Some women drape over their hair a large cloth sewn all over with silver and brass coins and shells, which jingle at every step they take. To procure such necessities as tea and barley, the nomads move south to the Tsangpo valley in the coldest months. Stalking about the few market towns, they are full of curiosity and admiration, some with nude babies protruding from the front opening of their sheepskins like kangaroos. They marvel at how so many people can live so close together without moving about. At the first sign of spring, they hurriedly depart toward the north, lest the weather should become too hot for them.

In comparison with their southern kin, the nomads are better fed, food from their livestock being plentiful. Their sheep and yaks provide them with protein, as do the gazelles and antelopes with which the land is teeming. Fat, in the form of butter, they take with their tea. For carbohydrates, they rely on barley. They have more than enough meat, milk, and sour milk, which they relish. Living a spacious life, with a self-contained economy in which a man owning one thousand sheep and two hundred yaks is probably only middle class, they are the happiest souls in Tibet.

A more settled and less fortunate people are the farmers. Tied down to the land they cultivate, and living in bondage to the nobility and landowners, the farmers are physically shorter and smaller than the nomads and lead a more cramped spiritual life. Despite a prevailing notion that Tibet is a non-agricultural country, some travelers estimate that no less than five-sixths of the people are occupied with the cultivation of the soil. The soil is alluvial, often composed of sand blown by the wind to form a layer over gravel and shingle. The color of the soil is light brown or grayish, according to its humus content, which in any case is poor enough. For fertilizer, human dung, ashes of cow dung, and sometimes the fine silt from flood waters are used. The farmer knows some of the rudiments of crop rotation and fallow, but he does not apply them systematically. Irrigation is poor, and the rain sets in too late. On his impoverished land, the Tibetan farmer grows, with the crudest implements, Tsam Pa, or barley (the staple food of Tibet); turnips; far too few potatoes, for which many soils are well suited; some peas as winter fodder for horses; and in lower altitudes wheat, buckwheat, and millet. Raising of beef and dairy cattle is a sideline of the farmer. But, as a result of centuries of underfeeding, almost exclusively on straw (except for the few rainy months starting at the middle of June), the cattle are a miserably degenerate breed. The small output of milk, butter, and curd (which is dried and looked upon as a delicacy) is therefore much prized by the rural community.

The farmer wears a dark brown or gray coat of homespun wool, a pair of trousers, and, when not working, boots of the same material. He prefers to wear one sleeve of his gown only, leaving the other dangling behind—a fashion which all Tibetans delight in. His wife is dressed in a dark sleeveless gown, folded double at the back, with a waistband. Under her coat she wears a petticoat but no trousers. Her dainty apron of colored horizontal stripes is the sign of puberty. Another sign is her headdress, a red forklike thing fastened on top of her hair, which is parted in the middle to form two long queues. The headdress is made of straw stuffing bound in red wool, on which are sewn imitation corals. Another form of headdress, popular in Tsang, is in the shape of an arc which spans the head from ear to ear. In former times, the headdress was so clumsy to remove that women had to wear it to bed.

The women see to every household duty from fetching water to preparing the tea. All Tibetans prefer the Szechuan tea to any other brand. The tea is first brewed thoroughly in a little water to which some soda is added. It is then mixed in a long wooden tube with more boiled water, salt, and butter, and is churned vigorously up and down for about five minutes by a long stick with a pad at its lower end, like the plunger of an air pump. For the poor, this brew serves both as a drink and as a soup to wash down their barley meal. For many of them, butter is too much of a luxury to be used in preparing the tea. A tiny piece of it is put into the cup at the time of drinking, and while drinking they take care to blow off the fat on the surface in order to use it later for kneading the barley flour.

Dressing becomes more elaborate with the town people—composed of traders, government employees, and craftsmen—and most elaborate with the women of noble families. The men of the towns wear cotton or silk shirts beneath their gowns and, rich or poor, they wear a tiny piece of turquoise on the lobe of the right ear as a sign of urbanity. On the left ear, traders and commoners wear a metal ring set with turquoise, while the noblemen and intellectuals wear a long pendant composed of a pearl set between two slender olive-shaped turquoises. Only nobles who have entered government service may curl their hair into the twin knots mentioned before; all others—nobles and commoners—are allowed to wear only a queue.

On festive occasions the urban women wear an open-collared silk shirt, mostly pink or green. For a noble lady nothing but silk or brocade is acceptable, and the apron she wears, with its rainbowlike pattern and gold brocade borders, can be truly beautiful. Her headdress, which is decorated with pearls and corals, may have cost a fortune. On her breast lies a silver- and gold-plated amulet box, about the size of a cigarette case, richly carved and adorned with rubies, turquoises, and even diamonds. A Tibetan lady, on festive days, can heap any amount of jewels and ornaments on herself. A fashion specialist would require several pages to do her justice.

A day's routine for high-class Tibetans may be summarized as follows: Rising between six and eight in the morning, they first do homage to the family gods. After washing the hands, the lord or the lady sprinkles clean water around, using a piece of peacock plume or a kind of Indian plant called *Tsa-Ku-Sha*, and repeats thrice: *"Om Ma Hum"* to purify the place. Then squatting, he or she starts reading scriptures, keeping at it for hours at a stretch and drinking innumerable cups of tea before attending to business.

It is the custom of all Tibetans to have two meals a day, one at ten o'clock in the forenoon and the other at about five or six in the afternoon. Despite the lavish scale on which Tibetans entertain guests, their private meals are fairly simple. The principal food for the rich and poor alike is barley, which may be taken kneaded with tea, wine, or water. To add relish, the middle class have dried mutton or beef and chilies, while the nobility have one or two Chinese dishes. Tibetans as a rule do not care much for vegetables, which some think are good only for animals. Meat suits their palates, but their religion forbids killing. However, as the Tibetan soil is poor and the climate rigorous, a strictly vegetarian diet is impracticable. So the Tibetans reason that for every Buddhist rule there must be exceptions to suit special conditions. But they kill only sparingly, generally such large animals as cattle or sheep. By sacrificing a few lives, they say, they save many lives. But to kill many small fishes to make a fine dish would be a sin.

The menu is the same in the evening. Only for the few gourmets, a rice or noodle soup, dressed with plenty of meat and vegetables, provides a welcome change. More reading of the scriptures or mantras occupies the evening. Sleep follows not long after dark, light being for many a luxury. Those who can afford light retire much later. Everyone prays for the protection of the god before laying his head on the pillow.

To the Tibetans the spiritual world is full of destructive forces and malicious elements. Among these are celestial beings to be found both indoors

*The well-to-do
exhibit their
best tents.*

*They look as fantastic as their mission is professed to be*

*A cavalry force rides past to a phantom war*

*An effigy
to be burnt in
a religious
service.*

The state oracle
Nai-Ch'ung in a
trance. Every twelfth year he stands
host to all major and minor oracles in and
around Lhasa.

The Black Hat dancers performing
a religious drama.

*Four masked boys afford comic relief
in a serious religious dance.*

*A group of the performers*

*The thousand-room thirteen-storied Potala, Vatican of
lamaism, towering over the surrounding plain.*

*The bathing season in Lhasa*

*Summer residence of the Dalai Lama in the Jewel Park*

*A picnic party in full swing*

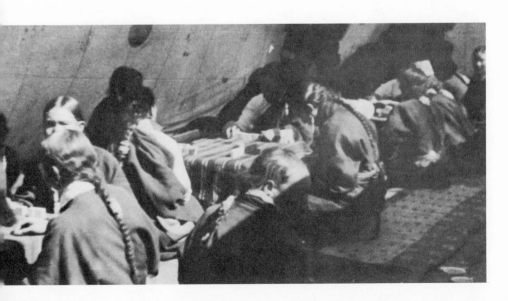

*Huge silk scroll of Buddha, which is unfurled once a year before a pious crowd*

and outdoors; the kings who reign over the five quarters\*; rulers of the air, of the water, and of the earth; and evil spirits who bring about tragic death. In addition, there is a vast army of "living ghosts" or witches (some of whom ride brooms), all harming humanity intentionally or unintentionally. On the other hand, there is the benign power of the Three Gems—Buddha, the Law, and the Priesthood.

Miracles abound in Tibet. From the Nying-Ma-Pa sect† originates the most potent propitiatory service. The patriarch of the Sa-Kya monastery holds sway over all witches in Tibet. When he begins the appropriate rites, the witches of the locality involuntarily start dancing and wailing into his presence. He even imposes a tax on them.

At the Zha-Lu monastery in Tsang, many monks lock themselves up in dark caves for life. Food is passed to them through small trap windows. Every twelve years, one of them lifts himself through the skylight by his mastery of *Lung* (the wind), and, dressed in a scarlet coat, a white apron, and a sash, with nimble feet he marches through all the principal towns in U and Tsang, covering a distance of over five hundred miles in seven days. All hurry to offer him money and scarves for his blessing. There is also the famous nun, within two-days' journey from Lhasa, who has been telling people's fortunes for the last three generations, and the dread mill in Se-Ra which, when it starts grinding, drips human blood, the blood of the cursed.

Tibetans could hardly live one minute without the protection of the Three Gems. They carry amulets and portable shrines about their body; they erect family altars to guard their rooms; and they build prayer walls, pagodas, temples, and monasteries to guard their villages and towns. They are constantly holding services to appease the gods, doing charity and penance to accumulate good deeds, and making pilgrimages to holy places. They recite endless scriptures, give endless offerings, and consult endless oracles.

They visualize in all phenomena the significant *Khor* (wheel). The world rotates in a Khor around Mount Sumeru; the sun and the moon rotate around the earth; all living beings rotate around the wheel of transmigration. Life is a perpetual circumambulation around some holy object, be it a holy peak, a holy lake, a holy pagoda, a holy wall, or a holy man. Let everything whirl around—the beads around the fingers, the prayer wheels around the sacred formulas. There are table wheels turned by the fingers; portable wheels turned by hand; tiny wheels turned by the winds; larger wheels propelled by man power; and the largest wheels of all, driven by hydraulic power. Wheels within wheels, whirling round and round. Imagine all the Tibetans

---

\* North, east, south, west, and center: namely, the universe.
† The leading red sect which specializes in rituals such as curing sickness and chasing demons.

muttering scriptures, counting beads, and turning prayer wheels, and continually walking round their monasteries, their cities, and their country where hundreds of thousands of such wheels are perpetually in motion; So this is Tibet.


## Polyandry and Connubial Perplexities

Polyandry, of the type in which several brothers share one wife, is a popular form of marriage in Tibet. In one family we know, one lady presides over a committee of seven husbands. How a husband's right is to be apportioned among the claimants varies with each family. Some tacit understanding based on rotation always exists. This is especially true among the commoners; with them there are always some absentee husbands out on pilgrimages or trading trips. Among the higher classes, precedence is automatically given to the most prosperous husband. The propensity to subordinate everything to rank and position seems innate in Tibetan noble blood. When a child is born, it is the most important spouse who gets the honor of being the father, the rest being mere uncles.

Blood plays only a minor part in the Tibetan family—especially in the male line. Thus, one prevalent system is called *Mar Pa* (the male bride). To be a Mar Pa is no disgrace, for this title designates one who marries into a family to become its legitimate heir. It would not be a strange custom if it were limited to families where male issue is wanting. In certain cases, however, there *is* a son, who is either passed over or is forced to become a monk in order to make way for the "male bride." We often heard that the ousted son was foredoomed by his horoscope to a short life and therefore gave himself up to a religious cause, and we discovered later that the Mar Pa in these cases was a stronger man.

A rather daring twist was given to the custom in one case where the master of an illustrious family died without leaving any issue and his widow decided to take in a Mar Pa. The lucky gentleman came into happy possession of a wife, a house, and a name. A Mar Pa, by becoming the heir of his wife's family, severs all relations with his own family. He takes his wife's family name and calls every relative of hers as she does.

The difficulty in determining individual relationships where so many complications arise is much simplified in the houses of the nobles. As we have pointed out, a Tibetan noble carries his titles into his family life. High dignitaries and their wives are always addressed by their respective titles even in the family circle. Words like father, mother, brother, sister, and so forth, do exist; but the vocabulary is deficient. When difficulties arise, word substitutes have to be found. For instance, in one case a woman with a son is married to two husbands who are not brothers but partners in business. For distinction, the son calls his older stepfather "senior father," and his younger one "junior father." In another case, a high noble falls in love with the wife of a lesser noble. The lady reciprocates the love but is not willing to divorce her husband. The trio find a happy solution when the lover decides to marry his ladylove along with her husband. Now the lady calls her husbands by their official titles and happily looks after the property of both.

But the most unusual case of all is that of a self-imposed Oedipus situation in which the father and the son of a most respectable house share the affections of one woman. The son was originally engaged to a girl of another respectable family. While the marriage was pending, the father, who was a widower, decided to take a wife. She came from a very rich family, and brought a considerable dowry—but she came on one condition: she did not wish her husband's son to marry a girl from outside lest one day she should be deprived of all property at her husband's decease. Therefore, the son was made to call off his engagement and to marry her instead. We do not know what has happened to these three persons, but when we left them the father seemed to be taking advantage of the bargain, and there were rumors of an impending revolution.

Property—how to preserve it, how to avoid its being divided up, and how to increase it—seems to underlie all these marital oddities. Monogamy, polygamy, polyandry, are not the right words for describing all the forms of alliances. Almost all forms are permissible so long as they further the family interests.

Still another interesting custom is the wholesale merger of two unrelated families into one. The opposite practice of splitting a family in two also occurs. But whether in one way or in another, economic considerations always dominate. For the noble families to divide or unite, government sanction is essential. Love and jealousy, which play so vital a role elsewhere, seem to have no claim in a Tibetan home.

Western writers have remarked on the free and respectable status of Tibetan womanhood. It is true that they do not bind their feet, nor do they observe purdah. And, as a rule, they control the family purse strings. However, Tibetan gentlemen do not bring chairs for their ladies, nor believe in "ladies first." There is no Tibetan equivalent for the "fair sex." Instead, women are called "the lower beings." A woman's place in Tibet is at home, propagating, keeping house, and running the shop. Higher aspirations are denied her. Politics ban her. Religion discriminates against her. She is considered to be carnal pleasure personified and hence to belong to a lower order.

In the lower field of worldly pleasure, women need suffer no inhibitions. They are courted, and they flirt before their own husbands. Wives can be bartered and hired out. They are playthings, though at the same time they play with others: they play with their own men; they play with the monks; they have even played with a few saints—often to the latter's ruin. An incarnation lama once confided to one of us: "Woman is woe!"

## A Ride in a Bridal Procession

In the small hours of a midsummer night, we rode through the muddy lanes of Lhasa to attend a Tibetan wedding. Important ceremonies take place in Tibet unusually early. Brides leave their homes before dawn as if eloping. Tibetans attach great importance to auspicious dates and hours, and the earliest hour in the day is deemed the luckiest. Thus, the astrologer had announced that the bride should be married off at four o'clock in the morning, and we rose at two to attend her wedding.

Not everybody can attend a Tibetan wedding. One has to respect the horoscopic laws, as we did in China. The presence of persons whose zodiacal signs clash with those of either the bride or the groom will bring disaster. To be safe, Tibetan weddings are held *in camera*. We were fortunate, for not only were we exempted from the rule but in order that we might witness the entire ceremony we were granted a "lift" in the bride's procession.

We arrived at the bride's home and found it dark and quiet. The servants told us that the bride was up and had begun her coiffure. They were going to light gas lamps at the family chapel where the ceremony would be observed. The chapel was one of the largest we had yet seen. In addition to the usual array of images and sacred books behind the lamps and offerings, which filled the upper end of the room, high seats and gilt tables had been arranged around a square space in the middle. Along the walls were hung rich painted scrolls, while bunches of silk scarves were tied on the pillars.

We were assigned to a corner of the spacious hall where we could watch the whole proceedings and were soon joined by a lama whose horoscopic reading tallied with the bride's. The lama was a learned man and helpfully communicative. Thanks to him, we came to know that the preliminaries of a Tibetan marriage follow much the same line as in China thirty years ago.

Proposals are made through go-betweens, and the horoscopes of bride and groom must be in harmony. When the parents give their consent, after consulting their children's opinions, a contract is drawn giving the terms on which the alliance is to be made.

Such a contract begins with a poetic eulogy of the happy event in prospect, and it goes on to give a short sketch of the betrothed pair, dwelling on their beauty and accomplishments, their attachment to each other, the complete harmony of their horoscopes, and the endorsement of their parents. Then follows the business side. The family which is going to receive either a bride or a "male bride" as a rule pays the opposite party a stipulated sum of what is known as "milk money"—an estimate of the amount expended for his or her upbringing. The same family also pays another sum to meet the expense of the engagement party on the occasion when both parties meet with the go-betweens to conclude the contract, an equivalent to our engagements.

On the other hand, the family which is going to marry off the son or daughter grants the bride a dowry, which—whether in the form of cash, goods, land, or slaves—is to be stated in an appended list. Then follow the provisos such as the complications of a Tibetan marriage call for. Seals are affixed by both families and the go-betweens to the end of the contract, and everything winds up in a song about the perfection of things.

But to return to the ceremony: The stage was set. In grave silence the family members filed in, in official robes, and seated themselves in order at the left of the altar. Then a person came in all muffled up in colored silk and brocade and heavy ornaments, and was supported by maidservants to a high raised seat facing the altar. She was heard sobbing behind the silk veil which covered her face. This was the bride.

Five servants came in, dressed in yellow brocade robes, on which was embroidered the design of a green sprawling dragon; red, flat-topped, wide-brimmed hats, trimmed with red tassels; and dark boots. They sat down beside the bride. Five more servants, similarly clad, were led in to the opposite seats by a priest in a yellow robe and a saucer cap. They were followed by four men in plain yellow silk, who seated themselves across from the bride's family. Our lama companion told us that the priest belonged to the old school, Nying-Ma-Pa sect, and the party following him had been sent the day before by the groom to fetch the bride.

A few minutes of silence passed. Two servants entered, one bearing a dish of barley flour bedecked with colored flags, the other a tray of barley grains. They were followed by three maids bringing in a huge jug of Tibetan wine, Ch'ang, and large silver cups. Starting with the head of the family, they served each in turn. The family members picked up some flour and grain between the finger tips, and, after tossing it in the air as a dedication, put the remnants into their mouths. When the wine came, they dipped their fourth fingers into it, flipped the wine in the air with their thumbs, and then put their fingers to their mouths.

After the servants retired, the priest started chanting a short scripture, in a low and long-drawn-out cadence. More servants came in to serve Tibetan tea, fruit, and rice. Each of the family made the same gestures as before.

Another intermission followed. The groom's party then lined up before the bride's family, while other servants brought in a small table laden with boiled mutton, beef, and rice, which were again served round in the symbolic fashion. Scarves were then placed around the necks of the groom's party, who started, in a low and monotonous chorus, a song praising the prosperity and glory of the bride's house. Standing erect in their places, they raised their hands before their breasts, jerking their arms up and down stiffly in their long flowing sleeves. Stamping their feet at the same time, they started a dance, like a row of dolls sprung into action. Wine and scarves were presented to the dancers, after which the members of the bride's family rose and gave a similar performance.

After a further exchange of scarves between the members of the two houses, all rose and accompanied the bride out of the hall. At a hint from our lama friend, we hurried downstairs just in time to see the bride squatting beside the pony that was to carry her to her new home. She was in a heap, weeping and sobbing. One of the groom's party was attaching an arrowlike object about four feet long to her back. This object, according to our informant, was called Da Dar. It was crowned by five points and draped in silk ribbons of five different colors—both the points and the ribbons standing for five blessings. A round mirror was suspended from it as a talisman against evil spirits. In ancient Tibet, a lover used to present a piece of turquoise to his ladylove as an emblem of possession. Now the turquoise has been replaced by the Da Dar, which the bride bears all the way to her groom.

Now the procession started. It consisted of the priest holding a painted scroll on a long willow branch—another talisman to scare off demons, the bride's escort, the bride, and the groom's party, all riding. We took up the rear at a respectful distance.

The mount for the bride was a gaily bedecked mare with a colt trotting beside her as a lucky omen. It took five attendants to support the bride while she sobbed and writhed in sore distress. Three times on the way the procession was accosted by welcoming parties from the groom. Wine was offered to the bride, and in the usual fashion dedicated to the god. When the pro-

*Tibet and the Tibetans*

cession reached the groom's house, a loud and glib singer sprang from nowhere and began to sing eulogies to the house. He sang about the gate, the house, the family chapel, the interior decorations, and many other things, before ending in praise of the prayer flags on the roof.

The procession stopped before the front steps of the house. There was no one to receive the bride. She was helped down onto a sort of platform heaped with leather bags of wheat, on top of which a swastika was drawn in grain. We followed her upstairs to the family chapel where the members of the house, including the groom, were seated in their official robes. No form of greeting passed between the bride and the groom or any of the family. She was conducted to a seat below her husband, and the Da Dar was put into a box of grain before the altar. Then all the rest of the procession filed in and sat down. The same dedication of wine and food and the same singing and dancing as we had witnessed in the bride's house followed.

From beginning to end, the exact ceremony was repeated. Toward its finish, the newlyweds led a small procession of attendants to the roof, the bride holding the Da Dar in her hands. A tent had been put up there in which a few lamas were chanting in slow rhythm. The couple walked around once, burning an incense herb called *Sang*. A new member had now been added to the family, and she was paying her first homage to the deity who looked after the house. The solemn affair was over. It was half-past five, and the sky was growing bright.

The groom's house was till then as bare of guests as the bride's had been. We were joined shortly, however, by a group of chatty and restless children. One of the small girls suddenly remarked to her friend:

"Look, the bride wasn't crying at all!"

"How do you know?"

"Look at her face—not a single tear!"

We looked at the bride. Her face was now uncovered. Her eyes met ours and were tearless indeed. She blushed at being seen at such close range. This experience taught us that Tibetans know how to play their parts admirably well.

## First and Last Rites of a Tibetan

A Buddhist divides a life's span into four stages: birth, growth, decadence, and extinction. While birth calls for no particular rejoicing, neither is death the occasion for any excess of sorrow.

Tibetans celebrate the birth of a child on the third day by small parties. Though girls are not ill received, boys are generally preferred. The moment a baby is born, a little mixture of barley flour and butter is put into its mouth as the first mouthful of food. A tiny piece of butter is laid on the vein on its crown to prevent "the wind," which, according to Tibetan doctors, is responsible for one-third of all human ailments. For the same purpose, a thick solution of butter is given to the mother. No special diet is prescribed for pregnant women or mothers. But, rich or poor, all Tibetan women prefer to nurse their own babies.

The baby gets a name on completion of its first month of life. The name may be given by the parent or, preferably, by a high lama. With few outstanding exceptions, there seems to be no distinction between the names of males and females. High lamas always give their own names to children as a blessing. That is why namesakes are so common among Tibetans. It is often on the name-giving day that babies are carried to temples on their first outings to give offerings to Buddha. Birthdays are not celebrated as a rule.

Children in Tibet were once brought up along Spartan lines. One old custom, surviving to this day, is that babies from two to three months old are stripped naked and put in the sun for hours, even in the coldest months. But before they are exposed, butter is rubbed thoroughly into the babies' skin and is not washed off after sunning. The practice, believed to ensure good resistance to the rigorous weather of Tibet, is continued two or three times a month till a child is two or three years of age.

In Tibet, as elsewhere, an important source of misery is sickness. Human sickness (of which there are four hundred four varieties, according to Buddhist pathology) is caused either by ignorance, by neglect, or by malignant influences.

When evil influences are at work, the only cure is through the power of the Three Gems. According to Tibetans, deities capable of doing harm dwell not only around us but even within us. There are, for example, five families of celestial spirits in each human body. One lives on top of the head, another above the right shoulder, a third and fourth under the armpits, and a fifth within the heart. The first is the most vital one. It must be identified by the astrologer in order to be propitiated constantly. The human soul, we are also told, travels around the body every day. One touch upon the point where it is resting can be fatal. Besides this, our horoscopes render us especially susceptible to certain evil influences abroad. Thus, for everyone there are certain moments, days, months, and years in which his life is in jeopardy.

On the other hand, quite a number of our physical disorders are brought about by our own ignorance and neglect. Hence, it is always wise to consult a lama. When he is satisfied that no evil influence is at work, he will counsel the use of medicine.

According to Buddhist classification, medical science is one of the ten subjects of human knowledge. Tibetan medical science, besides borrowing abundantly from China and India, is said to be based on an important work discovered long ago at Sam-Ye monastery. Many such works, covering a wide range of subjects, have been "discovered" in Tibet. They are alleged to be books written by gods or sages and hidden in secret places for the destined discoverer. This particular book is attributed to one Men-La, master of medicine, whose image is now to be seen at the medical college on the peak west of the Potala.

Tibetan medical science in its most advanced stage is said to be inseparable from the study of the occult influence of stars on human destiny. An expert, they say, is capable not only of diagnosing what is physically wrong with his patient but also of reading his fortune and that of his close relatives. In the more unpleasant aspects of medicine, however, a Tibetan physician prescribes many mystic recipes, which may mean anything from a living Buddha's tea, food, or hair down to his excrement.

When neither divine help nor medicine proves of any use, it means that the disorder is caused by destiny, and is inevitable.

When death occurs, the astrologer is consulted as to where and on what object the mind of the deceased rested in the last minute, what prayers are to be offered, which of the family members are to keep away from funeral ceremonies because of horoscopic disharmonies, and the appropriate date and time for the funeral, as well as the direction in which the funeral journey is to begin.

For forty-nine days, the Tibetans believe, the soul of the departed is kept in a state of "middle being"—a state intervening between this life and the next. The family keeps up a fire in a crockery vessel suspended in the deceased's room, and three times a day a mixture of barley, butter, sugar, and sandalwood or other spices is poured into it. The "middle being," since it is bodiless, cannot subsist on substantial foods but only on fumes and odors. A learned lama is invited to recite a special scripture to clear the way for the soul to its next round in the wheel of transmigration. Sometimes a holy letter must be written and placed on a certain part of the corpse to prevent the straying soul from re-entering it. For, if that should happen, the corpse might rise and do havoc among the living. That is the reason, some have told us, why the doors are so low and the stairs so precipitous in a Tibetan house—to prevent a revived corpse from chasing the living too fast.

When the preliminaries are done, the undertaker comes to do his gruesome job. To Tibetans the body from which the soul has gone deserves no solicitude. It is stripped, the spine is broken in two, and the body is doubled up with the head between the knees. It is then bound with white cloth and placed behind a cloth partition in a corner. A five-cornered crown is put on its head. Tibetans think this is the way it came into the world. Butter lamps and offerings are placed before it while a number of lamas, preferably of the occultist school, keep vigil day and night, chanting incessant prayers.

Very few come to pay their last respects. Still fewer are allowed to enter the room where the remains are. To show condolence, it is enough to present a silk scarf with some money in it to pay for holding prayers or painting a portrait of the deceased's patron deity. The clothes and belongings of the deceased are offered to the lamas in return for their special prayers.

To dispose of the corpse, four methods are known in Tibet. For the destitute class, the corpse is thrown into a river or sunk with a piece of heavy stone. This custom is now proscribed by law, though still practiced at out-of-the-way places. Those who are suspected of having died of infectious diseases are buried in the earth. But this is not popular. A third mode of disposal is cremation. When this is prescribed by high lamas, the corpse is first burned in a closed oven. Then the ashes are scraped up, mixed with clay, and molded into hundreds of tiny pagodas. These are dumped in heaps over the countryside as a last dedication to the Three Gems.

But the most popular method is called *Ja-Tor*, meaning "feeding the birds." A peculiar species of bird, a smaller and uglier version of ostrich, which the Tibetans name *Ja-Gor*, through the ages has learned to live near the areas set aside for Ja-Tor. There are innumerable such spots in Tibet.

We once ventured to one of these places. It was before sunrise when we arrived at a desolate rocky place that would make a perfect setting for a murder story. Two suspicious-looking men seated on a piece of rock were having their breakfast. A monk with a lantern sat a little distance off. We approached him and learned that it was a lama, his own spiritual teacher, who was going to be cut up for the birds. There was a white bundle lying on a huge boulder about fifty feet off. We walked some distance away in trepidation.

The men started burning sandalwood, the aroma of which, as we learned later, aroused the birds high up among the rock caves. The men unbound the corpse and began the job, grinding the bones into bits and kneading them with barley. The birds swooped down in batches, about a hundred or so, walking and chattering noisily a good distance off. We retreated farther away.

The disciple looked on. Within half an hour everything was gone. Had anything been left behind, the disciple would certainly have deemed it a bad sign. Only the bodies of the condemned, it is believed, are shunned by the birds. But now he was satisfied. His master had given away everything. What else could be desired?

For a few top-ranking incarnation lamas, there is still another form of burial. The remains, having been dried and cured with salt, are embalmed, wrapped in five-colored silks, and enshrined in a pagoda. Such a pagoda is an object for common worship. The gold pagodas of the Dalai Lama in the Potala and the silver ones of the Panchen Lama in Tra-Shi Lun-Po are the most illustrious examples. Salt water which drips from the corpse is mixed with clay and is made into tiny images of Buddha. Miraculous powers are attributed to these images. Those who are fortunate enough to get them cherish them in those pretty charm boxes they carry around their necks or above their heads to give them divine protection.

# part six

## All Year Round in Lhasa

### In the Shadow of the Potala

A Tibetan friend once warned us that those who had seen Lhasa would always miss it. We have since realized how true it is.

By modern standards, Lhasa, this so-called Vatican of Buddhism, is a mere village, less than two miles from east to west and about one mile from north to south. It lies in a stretch of the east-west valley of the river Chi-Ch'u. Though it is situated in the heart of the "Land of Snow," there is here no snow peak in view. The town is surrounded by hills from four to five thousand feet high, all bare and craggy, which in the fanciful eyes of the local inhabitants assume the shapes of the "Eight Precious Emblems." A shower or a chilly wind in the Lhasa valley during the "rainy season," from June to August, often brings a spray of white to most of the hilltops. When you labor up one of these heights, some of the famous snow ranges of Tibet will loom in view. Otherwise, you do not feel that you are already on a level with the highest peaks in Europe. The sky is eternally blue, and consequently the sun, the moon, and the stars are glorious. The climate throughout the best part of the year is mild and for many months is pleasant.

Pleasant in the eyes of Tibetans must be the valley which is lulled by the music of the Chi-Ch'u, the "Water of Pleasure." The river has points here nearly one mile wide at full stream and meanders through the southern out-skirts of the city along a "green belt." Except in the rainy months, when the river is swollen to a muddy and boisterous stream, it runs its bluish-crystal course along sandy banks, adding a lively note to the peaceful countryside. The "green belt"—composed of meadows, shrubs, and groves along the river embankment bearing the name of a Chinese Amban, Chang—is called in Tibetan *Ling-Ka* (garden). For it is a garden to the inhabitants of the arid, treeless city, and brings them the lush cooling breath of an oasis. A few private gardens have sprung up lately with somewhat modern trimmings. However, the greatest part of Ling-Ka remains in its natural condition and is open to all.

Tibetans say that all ways lead to Lhasa. But the best approach, during the warmer months at least, is from the west. After passing the foot of Dre-Pung monastery, you come on a vast expanse of green turf, over which rears in the distance the right shoulder of a Potala from an outcrop of rock. Toward the right sprawls a rather extensive grove encircled by a low wall. Amid the trees, you get glimpses of a golden roof. That is the Nor-Bu Ling-Ka (the Jewel Park) of the Dalai Lama, at the western end of the green belt.

A small and ill-defined road meets you after you cross the green field—small at parts even by Tibetan standards, and ill-defined it must appear to every stranger. To the people of Lhasa, however, it is the holy walk, Ling-Kor (the Outer Circle), which loops around the main portion of Lhasa. Cutting between the Nor-Bu Ling-Ka and Lhasa, it embraces an old monastery named Kun-De-Ling, in which resides an incarnation lama of the rank qualified for regency. This monastery forms, with three others, a venerable group called Ling-Zhi (the Four Monasteries), from which have come several regents.

Right behind Kun-De-Ling and over a little rise is the temple commemo-rating Ke-Sar, the Chinese hero of a central Asian saga bearing his name. He is somehow mixed up by the Tibetans with the legendarized knight, Kuan Yu, immortalized in the famous Chinese novel *The Three Kingdoms*. It would be extremely interesting to see why and how this popular Chinese hero of the second century was first canonized by the Manchu dynasty and later con-nected with the Tibetan Ke-Sar, whose home has been established as being in modern Sikang.

Suppose we follow the Ling-Kor in the proper direction between a sand dune and a running brook toward the rear of the Potala. Here is another landmark, Lu-Khang (House of the Dragon). Girdled by a wall and sur-rounded by a profusion of giant poplars and gnarled willows is an emerald pond mirroring the northern façade of the Potala. An islet is in the middle with a temple in which are enshrined the Dragon Gods. Many traditions

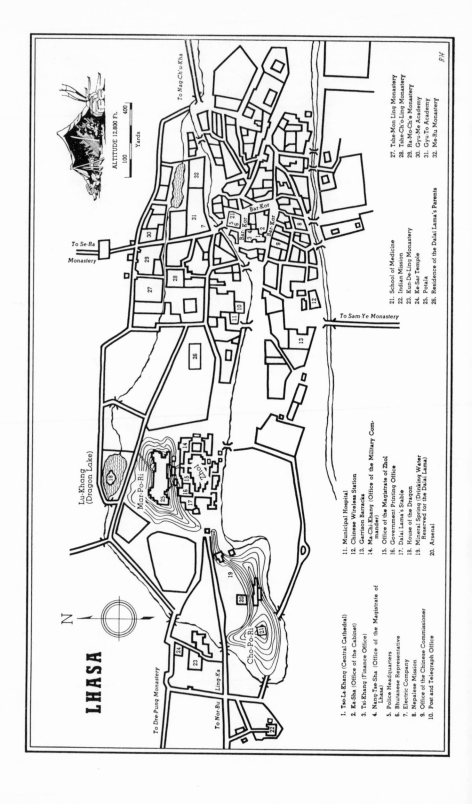

# LHASA

N

ALTITUDE 12,800 Ft.

Yards
100    400

To Nag-Ch'u-Kha

To Se-Ra
Monastery

To Sam-Ye Monastery

To Dre-Pung Monastery

To Nor-Bu Ling-Ka

Lu-Khang
(Dragon Lake)

Mar-Po-Ri

Cho-Po-Ri

Bar-Kor

1. Tso-L-Khang (Central Cathedral)
2. Ka-Sha (Office of the Cabinet)
3. Tsi-Khang (Finance Office)
4. Nang-Tse-Sha (Office of the Magistrate of Lhasa)
5. Police Headquarters
6. Bhutanese Representative
7. Electric Company
8. Nepalese Mission
9. Office of the Chinese Commissioner
10. Post and Telegraph Office

11. Municipal Hospital
12. Chinese Wireless Station
13. Garrison Barracks
14. Ma-Chi-Khang (Office of the Military Commander)
15. Office of the Magistrate of Zhol
16. Government Printing Office
17. Dalai Lama's Stable
18. House of the Dragon
19. Mineral Spring (Drinking Water Reserved for the Dalai Lama)
20. Arsenal

21. School of Medicine
22. Indian Mission
23. Kun-De-Ling Monastery
24. Ke-Sar Temple
25. Potala
26. Residence of the Dalai Lama's Parents

27. Tshe-Mon Ling Monastery
28. Tshe-Ch'o-Ling Monastery
29. Ra-Mo-Ch'e Monastery
30. Gyu-Me Academy
31. Gyu-To Academy
32. Me-Ru Monastery

in Tibet tell about the existence of seas in prehistoric times in the highland. The Dragons, who rule the water and can raise storms and cause inundations, are an especially dreaded family of gods in Tibet. Either because of this or because its exuberant verdure is too much for the stoic Tibetan taste, this beautiful place is visited by the people of Lhasa only once a year. But we are told that, because of its convenient position and its shady seclusion, it was once the favorite rendezvous for the Sixth Dalai Lama in his amorous adventures.

Leaving the House of the Dragon, the holy walk skirts the northern portion of the city, where we pass the ancient monastery Ra-Mo-Ch'e, said to have been founded by the Tang princess Wen Chen in the seventh century. To the left, within two miles across an undulating field, a great cluster of buildings comes into view at the foot of the northern hill. It is Se-Ra monastery. Fanning out on the barren hills behind Se-Ra are a number of hermitages. Though looking unpretentious from a distance, some are lovely and commodious retreats, once homes of culture, founded by the pundits whose names they still bear. Many important buildings are centered in the northern section of the city. Two are especially important. One is Tshe-Mon-Ling monastery, ranked as one of the Ling-Zhi, and the other, Me-Ru monastery, a name as ancient and as inexplicable as Sam-Ye monastery. The other two Ling, which might be mentioned here, are Tshe-Ch'o-Ling on the opposite bank of the Chi-Ch'u, the least important of the four, and Ten-Gye-Ling in the heart of the city, which was destroyed by the Thirteenth Dalai Lama in a political strife.

Having traversed the northern section, the Ling-Kor turns south to enclose the east end of the city, where the old bazaar is situated. Spreading into many lanes which intersect this part, the market is composed of small shops and roadside stalls where everything from daily provisions to mules and ponies can be had. Business is brisk every morning, when the place is full of noise and colors and thronging with men and animals.

The road then bends west, cutting between the town proper and green parks south along the river, until it reaches the foot of a cone-shaped hill on the west. This hill is called Cho-Po-Ri (Iron Hill), which, together with Mar-Po-Ri (Red Hill), on which the Potala stands, comprise the two humps which can be seen from both ends of the Lhasa valley. The road carves a footpath along the outer edge of the hill, turning it into by far the most picturesque section of the holy walk. All along the rock surface are carved and painted images of gods, and beside the path are devotional pieces of carved granite with colored images and mantras, some displaying remarkable workmanship. The surrounding groves and stream and the view of the Chi-Ch'u river add further charm to the spot. Turning north between the grounds of Nor-Bu Ling-Ka and Kun-De-Ling monastery, we come to the foot of the little mound on which is located the temple of Ke-Sar. This completes the six-mile circle of the famous Ling-Kor.

The entrance to Lhasa proper leads straight from this point. Advancing toward the east, we see Mar-Po-Ri and the top of the Potala in front of us, and to the right, crested by a yellow circular building, the school of medicine. Now we see that the twin peaks are connected by a low sagging ridge, at the lowest point of which has been opened a gate to Lhasa. Much consternation was once caused by the breakthrough at the middle of the "Dragon," which has its head at Mar-Po-Ri and its curled tail at Cho-Po-Ri. The construction of three imposing pagodas, one astride the gateway, joining the other two, one on either side, by a festoon of tinkling bells, restored the dragon's back-bone and forestalled a sure calamity to Tibet.

Cho-Po-Ri has a slight advantage in height over Mar-Po-Ri, but the thir-teenth story of the Potala, in which the Dalai Lama resides, exceeds it suffi-ciently to uphold the rule that no one must look down upon the Dalai. The Potala is seen to its best advantage when, after we pass through the gate of the middle pagoda, it swings into full view with its massive façade towering over four hundred feet high. A small village, *Zhol*, nestles below it. There a magistrate resides whose jurisdiction extends over all the surrounding regions of Lhasa.

Our road leads right below the Potala, across open ground before the massive gate of the village. To the right stands a monolith, one of the most ancient relics of Tibet. Few Tibetan scholars can read its text, which is an oath of allegiance between the king Khri-Son De-Tsan and his courtiers, transacted at the peak of the Tibetan empire. On the left are two yellow pavilions, each sheltering a quadrilingual monument. The pavilions are yellow because the monuments record royal rescripts. One concerns the pacification of Tibet during the time of the Junkar invasion by Emperor Kang Hsi, and the other concerns the victory over the Gurkhas by Emperor Chien Lung. At the northeast corner of Mar-Po-Ri, the generals who took part in the Junkar campaign have also recorded their achievement on the rocky face of the hill.

On the way to Lhasa the road crosses a stone bridge with green glazed tiles and enclosed windows. Much superstition clings to this Chinese archi-tecture. Those who leave Lhasa must not pass it, whereas those who are arriving may safely do so. Nobody knows why, but everybody conforms. The remains of another gate guard the entrance to the town. A little farther and we come to Bar-Kor, "the Middle Circle."

Bar-Kor is a rather broad street that girdles an irregular square where the all-important Central Cathedral, Tsu-La-Khang, is located. The street is less than a mile long and is the site of a flourishing new bazaar. Besides the part occupied by the cathedral and by a few homes of old noble families, both sides of the street are lined with shops, some of which might even be called modern. Owing to its location as well as its convenient length, it is by far the most popular holy walk for the inhabitants of Lhasa.

The building of the cathedral, initiated by the Nepalese queen of Son-Tsan Gam-Po, is associated with many legends. The most famous concerns the removal of an underground sea from Lhasa to Koko Nor lake. Another relates the selection of the site by the Chinese Princess Wen Chen, who saw in the topography of the Lhasa valley the likeness of an ogress lying on her back. The cathedral has been demolished and rebuilt many times and stands as a rallying point for Buddhism in Tibetan history. Though laden with thousands of images and a millennium and a half of growing traditions, this three-story structure, with its gate facing west, is rather unimposing. In front of the gate is a venerable-looking willow, which according to one tradition was planted by Princess Wen Chen of Tang. It certainly looks very old, though how old no one can tell. The people of Lhasa call it "the Lord's Hair, which conveys a good idea of its leafy spread. Under the tree is a monolith with a Chinese-Tibetan version of a treaty of friendship signed between Ta Tang and Tibet in 822. Another bilingual stone monument stands right before the gate of the cathedral. It contains what is usually known as the "Smallpox Edict," issued by a very energetic Chinese Amban in the last decade of the eighteenth century. It seeks not only to stop the Tibetan practice of banishing those afflicted with smallpox, advocating vaccination instead, but also to proscribe the custom of cutting up corpses to feed the birds, a most hideous custom from a Chinese viewpoint. Many scars on the monument bear witness to the Tibetans' resentment of the interference. Behind this monument are more tablets giving a detailed account of the victory over the Gurkhas, together with names of the higher-ranking officers who took part in the campaign. There are more tablets along the right wall of the gate containing royal edicts by Emperor Tao Kwang on the determination of the Dalai and the Panchen incarnations by the drawing of lots from a golden urn.

The central figure in the Central Cathedral is the celebrated image of Sakya Muni at twelve years of age, which was brought from China by Princess Wen Chen. Many other interesting images are enshrined there, including those of a trio consisting of the king Son-Tsan Gam-Po and his Chinese and Nepalese consorts. Within the compound of the cathedral, which is an indescribable agglomeration of small chapels and corridors, is the shortest holy walk, called Nang-Kor (the Inner Circle). Many prayer wheels line the walk, as do innumerable mural paintings devoted to legends of Lord Buddha. Part of the outer wing of the premises has been appropriated for government use. A door opens to the south on a stone courtyard and a dais, on which Gan-Dan Khri-Pa, "the pope," preaches during the New Year festivals.

North of the cathedral is the office for the magistrates of Lhasa. The northern section of the new bazaar is exclusively a Nepalese colony, all shops there being run by the tribesmen of Nepal. Mohammedans, mostly from Chinghai with a few from India, predominate in the other sections, which contain a sprinkling of Chinese shops, while Tibetans monopolize the stalls along both sides of the road.

Four tall flagpoles mark roughly the four quarters of the main street of Lhasa, each possessing a name and an individual significance. One flagpole governs Tibet's political fortune, another its religious prosperity, the third bestows individual happiness, and the fourth a successful career. Once every year the poles are leveled, strengthened, adorned with new prayer flags, and then re-erected with much ceremony.

Unpaved, unlit, dirty, and with an abundance of dogs guarding their respective spheres of influence, Bar-Kor is also the scene of many revelries and festivities throughout the year. It is not only the main street of Lhasa but also the only real street in all Tibet. Yet, the people there treat it unkindly. They dump their rubbish in it, and they use it as a public latrine. At the same time it is their holy walk, where a crowd turns up every evening to accumulate merits for this life and the next.


## The Month of a Hundred Thousand Merits

The Tibetan calendar, though based on Buddhist conception of "The Wheel of Time," bears the unmistakable influence of the Chinese lunar calendar. Very often the two completely coincide, lagging, roughly, from one to one and a half months behind the Gregorian calendar.

Like the Chinese, Tibetans count their years by matching the five elements against the twelve zodiacal signs, thus making one complete cycle every sixty years. The system, though apparently in use in earlier times, was perfected as late as the eleventh century, as may be proved by the fact that Tibetans claim that the current cycle is their sixteenth. But with typical Tibetan love of originality, they have tampered with the calendar, making additions and subtractions freely, such as duplicating dates which are deemed auspicious and omitting those which are inauspicious. Thus you may find, say, February 2 twice in succession and no date between February 3 and February 5. In each month the day of full moon and that of the new moon, the fifteenth and the thirtieth days, as well as the dates lying in between—the eighth and the twenty-third—are considered special days, on which our meritorious or wrong deeds possess extraordinary potency. All Tibet goes meatless on these days, butchering being officially banned. Tibetans have adopted the seven-day week but observe their rest day on Saturday. On that day no important business is to be transacted, no money paid out, and nothing taken out of storage rooms. All government offices declare it a holiday.

For convenience we shall not start our account of the Tibetan year with the New Year but with the beginning of the warm season, the third Tibetan month. In Tibet, as in all places along the Himalayan belt, only two seasons are noticeable in each year: the warm and the cold. When the dismal dust storms die away and the packed programs of the Tibetan New Year come to an end, Lhasa stirs with the first earnest breath of spring. Two events in Lhasa herald the arrival of the warm season. On the eighth day of the third month, the whole ecclesiastical and secular court rides in winter garments to a ceremony in the Potala and returns mysteriously changed into summer uniforms. The ceremony, besides being an official acknowledgment of the change of the season, is one of the three occasions each year when candidates for government service are initiated into office. Not long after this, on an auspicious day, comes the other event, when the Dalai Lama moves in state from his winter quarters in the Potala to his summer residence at Nor-Bu Ling-Ka. Needless to say, the procession is attended with all the pomp and pageantry befitting his importance. Monk and lay officials turn up with an escort of the Tibetan army for the Dalai Lama, who rides in a palanquin of yellow silk, borne by sixteen men. The event affords a double occasion for sightseeing to the people of Lhasa, for, on the day before, a full dress rehearsal is staged.

Every Tibetan heart warms at the fourth month, the month of the star Sa-Ka. This is a blessed month, for in this month Lord Buddha was born and in it he attained Nirvana and Buddhahood. The month is thus possessed of so much potency that the effect of anything, either good or bad, that one does then is multiplied a hundred thousand times.

Is it to be wondered at that the people of Lhasa should be so devoted to the accumulation of merits when virtue pays such high dividends? The whole month is declared a meatless month, since the taking of one life would then be equal to the taking of a hundred thousand lives. Only the Dalai Lama may have meat if he chooses. From the first day of the month, the devout start penance. Some abstain from food and drink every day from sunrise till sunset, and many observe silence for a period of eight days, fifteen days, or the whole month. Special prayers and lectures by high lamas are organized throughout the city. Dedications and offerings are redoubled. Lamps are lit before every altar. Each government minister grants amnesty to one prisoner serving life sentence. People who can save no human life buy sheep to save them from the butchers. Charity is poured upon the beggars, and mendicant monks and nuns flock from far and near. Some come with their tents and others with their shrines. Many sit quietly beside the Ling-Kor, turning their prayer wheels and muttering the scriptures. A few sit beside a running stream, dipping their water prayer wheels into the current. Others sit in rows, chanting in unison and clapping their hands vehemently. Everyone is looking for charity, which comes in the form of alms, barley flour, salt, and, curiously, even Tibetan wine, Ch'ang, all distributed by individuals or public bodies.

By far the most popular way to acquire merit is to walk the Ling-Kor. From the first day of the month, men and women, rich and poor, nobles and commoners are busy at the circumambulation around Lhasa. Whole families are out—husband, wife, children, and servants—all turning their prayer wheels and beads and being followed by their pet dogs and "redeemed" sheep. Then come the more zealous ones to whom walking is not enough. They come to do full prostration. First they fold their hands above the head; then, moving their hands down to the mouth and the breast, they measure their full length on the ground, with both arms stretched forward, placing a stone or piece of bone to mark the point the fingers reach. Then getting up, they repeat the same process, beginning from the last point. About a week's time is required to complete one round of the Ling-Kor in this fashion, and to do the job one has to put thick padding on the knees, and hide or leather gloves on the hands for protection against the rough ground. To some, measuring one's length is still not enough. They must measure their breadth the whole distance, going through the process crosswise. Once or twice we had the good fortune to admire a few who were performing this feat along steep rough paths on the side of the cone-shaped Cho-Po-Ri. And, though we have heard that in former times a number of pilgrims measured their length the whole way from Inner Mongolia to Lhasa, we challenge anybody's having measured his breadth the same distance.

A beautiful informal festival marks the fifteenth of the month. It takes place at the House of the Dragon when Lhasa pays its annual visit to the lovely pond. At this one time each year, the emerald water reflects the gaiety and colors of a holiday crowd. Wine shops and food shops spring up. Picnic parties are everywhere. Happy crowds throng the shady grassy banks to watch the fun. Soft music floats from the islet. A few hide boats are plying about, and ladies and gentlemen rush for a ride to the temple. In the scramble a few slip into the water, arousing roars of laughter.

On the same day the whole body of the secular officials, in their brilliant silk costumes, are led by the four ministers to walk a round of the Ling-Kor. They begin early in the morning with a service at the Central Cathedral. Then, starting from the northern section, near Ra-Mo-Ch'e monastery, they slowly wend their way through the east and south parts of the city; and after paying visits to Nor-Bu Ling-Ka and the Potala, they, too, come to ride in the hide boats. Every boat is then brimful of the colors of crimson, amber, and purplish silk, like flowers on the surface of the water. The ministers preside over a small ceremony in the House of the Dragon and sink five treasures into the lake as a dedication. Then they continue their walk until they reach the starting point, where they disperse.

But merriment is not limited to the pond and to Lhasa. Just a few hours walk east of Lhasa, a "flower offering" festival is observed, where both the state oracle Nai-Ch'ung and the patron protector of Tshe-Ch'o-Ling monastery are invited to give their prophecies. The latter oracle returns to Tshe-Ch'o-Ling the following day, when many Lhasa people ferry across the Chi-Ch'u to pay their homage. As we have said elsewhere, this is the best time to read one's visions on the famous Nam Tso lake.

We cannot conclude our chapter on the Month of a Hundred Thousand Merits without telling a story we heard about walking the Ling-Kor:

Once the Great Fifth Dalai Lama with much amazement saw from the heights of the Potala that the goddess Drol-Ma was walking the Ling-Kor. If he had seen it only once or twice, he would not have been surprised, since he was holy and subject to visions. But when he saw it every day at the same hour, he knew it must be a portent. He confided the matter to his followers, with instructions to investigate.

A few days later, they brought before him a poor shriveled old man, who shook from head to feet in fear before the Incarnation of Avalokitesvara. His Holiness smiled compassionately at him and inquired:

"Are you the man who often walks the Ling-Kor at this time of the day?"

"It is so, my Precious Savior, thou All-knowing, Almighty God. . . ." While making his admission, the man was babbling honorifics for his god king.

"Then do you know that every time you walk, Drol-Ma, the gracious goddess, is keeping watch over you?"

The old man stared and, putting out his tongue, groveled on the ground, moaning, gasping, and whining all at once, to the amusement of everyone, even the Great Fifth.

"Tell me, do you know it?"

"Oh, no, no!" The poor man shook his head in mortal fear of having been caught in a sacrilegious act. He moaned and knocked his head on the ground, begging for mercy.

"Now, don't fear," kindly admonished the Great Fifth. "Only tell me what you recite every time you do the holy walk. Is it the mantra, Om Ma Ni Pa Me Hum, or the scripture of Dedication to the Merciful Goddess?"

"Yes, it is the scripture of Drol-Ma, Drol-Ma the Goddess," answered the man, trembling. And he took courage to add that this was in fact the only scripture he had learned by heart since he had started walking the Ling-Kor forty years ago.

"Ah, very well. Now calm yourself. Can you recite it once to me? You have nothing to fear from me, old man. I want to hear you once, and I shall set you free."

It took several minutes for the man to become reconciled to the proposal. When he finally recited the scripture, he might have made the palace rock with laughter but for the revered presence of the Dalai Lama. But even His Holiness could not suppress a smile when he said:

"But, poor man, what a blunder! How can you have recited Drol-Ma all wrong for forty years without anybody in Lhasa telling you so?"

At the sternness of the remark, the poor fellow once more put out his tongue and sobbed and whined bitterly, giving himself up for lost.

"Stop!" interrupted the Great Fifth. "Now listen, for this time I shall be your teacher. I shall teach you how to recite Drol-Ma properly. And you people around me had better start teaching more seriously instead of laughing at such a poor old man!'

It took His Holiness the whole afternoon to correct the old man's mistakes and make him recite the proper text of Drol-Ma. After that the goddess Drol-Ma was not seen, even though, as the Great Fifth ascertained, the old man was performing his daily walk and recitation correctly.

The Fifth Dalai Lama, therefore, caused the old man to be brought before him once more, urged him to recite the text, and found that he could do so correctly. But why, His Holiness wondered, had Drol-Ma failed to reappear? After deep thought, he ordered the old man not to recite the correct text in future, but to recite it as he had been doing for the past forty years.

The next day, when His Holiness looked out from the Potala, once again he saw the gracious goddess Drol-Ma moving around the Ling-Kor. He instantly sent for the old man, and asked:

"Today, did you recite Drol-Ma in your own way or in the way I taught you?"

"My way—I mean, the wrong way."

"Then why does Drol-Ma, the goddess, grace you when you recite the wrong text but fail to appear when you do it right?"

Frightened again, the old man babbled, "I don't know, thou Almighty Precious Savior, I don't know. . . ."

"But I know," slowly commented His Holiness. Turning to his court, he explained: "When he recites the wrong text, his mind is concentrated on Drol-Ma, and the goddess comes to bless him. But when he recites the correct text, his mind is occupied with the text. That makes all the difference."

The moral of the story is: You don't have to *know* what is right as long as you *do* what is right.

## The Picnic Season in Lhasa

To the citified people of Lhasa, the mention of camping and picnics in the Ling-Ka brings the balm of the woods and the meadows. The Ling-Ka season begins in the fourth Tibetan month, and everybody in Lhasa talks about picnics until the end of the eighth month.

Looking back on our days in Lhasa, we cannot recollect any pleasanter days of relaxation than those when we joined the Tibetans in their outdoor pleasures. Neither can we forget how, on our first arrival in Lhasa, we deplored the lack of green in the town and how gradually we came to look upon those few acres of grass that border the river with an affection equal to that felt by the Lhasa people.

The Tibetans of Lhasa today have lost many of the traits of their forebears who selected Lhasa as the spot from which to rule a vast empire. The nobles, especially, have urban habits and tastes sophisticated under the Mandarin influence; thus, they have lost their links with nature, and the custom of Ling-Ka going is fast dying out among them. For outing, they go to their country homes. Their gardens are laid out in geometrical patterns. Their flowers are grown in pots. Their tents, if they live in tents at all, are so lavishly appointed that they cease to be tents. Twice we have seen such elaborate fabrications. One was a Mongolian tent, which looked not unlike an open parachute. The outside was covered with gold and green designs, while the interior was fully lined with red brocade and rich Tibetan carpets.

The other fabrication was a portable house, complete with windows, doors, and curtains, and raised on a wooden floor enclosed by a low wall. Both tents were stacked with tea tables, sofas, couches, cigarette stands, and carpets. And both had to be put inside a bigger tent for protection against the wind and rain.

It is among the common folks that one sees the best tradition of nomadic life kept alive. For three days, from the fourteenth to the sixteenth of the fifth month, the town pours out its inhabitants to the green acres along the Water of Pleasure. But it is on the fifteenth that the crowd is greatest. This is the "Day of the World's Offering of Joy," a day of thanksgiving.

Its origin is remote. In the old times, three offertory services were organized at various places in southern Tibet devoted to the "Three Baskets of Buddhism" (Buddha's sermons, the commentaries, and the disciplinary rules). Now only the service for the first of these is still observed, at Sam-Ye monastery. This is the occasion when all the lesser deities of the world descend on Sam-Ye to partake in the rejoicing. At this time pyres of the scented herb *Sang* are burned by the devout all over Tibet to welcome them.

One of the chief celestial visitors to Sam-Ye on this occasion is Tsi-Mar-Wa, the guardian deity of the monastery and the governor of all souls departed from the world. Ch'or Je, the living medium of Tsi-Mar-Wa, gives prophecies on the same day. After drinking the blood of a sacrificed sheep and smearing his face with it, he dances in a trance on the roof of the temple in iron-shod boots. According to Tibetan pundits, Tsi-Mar-Wa does not visit only Sam-Ye. He also pays a yearly visit to Lhasa, but, curiously, through the medium of another deity, the famed Ka-Ma-Sha.

Now Ka-Ma-Sha, the oracle of Se-Ra monastery, occupies a place in popular esteem second only to that of the so-called state oracle of Tibet, Nai-Ch'ung. Open rivalry exists between the two oracles. Son of a most dreaded legendary dragon in India, the deity Ka-Ma-Sha is a powerful follower of another Indian deity associated with Se-Ra. According to one version he is also the local deity of Lhasa. Twice a year he gives public prophecies, one on the thirtieth of the sixth month and the other near the end of the year. On the first occasion, the oracle dictates a list of daily articles and, having collected all of them and paraded once from Se-Ra to Lhasa, he publishes a statement of the symbols, together with his prophecies. His riddles never fail to wrack many a sagacious Tibetan brain.

On the fifteenth day of the fifth month, Ka-Ma-Sha, wearing gala dress and accompanied by a subordinate oracle, a lesser local deity, appears in the eastern suburb of Lhasa. Nothing seems easier than the invocation of the holy spirits by their respective mediums. Having partaken of some

Tibetan wine, both quickly work themselves into a frenzy, in which one throws two pairs of crossed swords in the air. Each is then helped to a dais. Here the two magistrates of Lhasa come to consult them, on behalf of the people of Lhasa, about the city's fortunes in the year to come. The first oracle to give prophecy through the medium of Ka-Ma-Sha is the deity Tsi-Mar-Wa.

The event draws huge crowds. However, even more people prefer to go to the riverbank to make offerings. Family parties and groups of relatives, friends, and neighbors parade along the waterside, all in their best attire and carrying bundles of the aromatic herb Sang, carpets, and baskets full of food and drink. They make a small pile of the scented herb below festoons of colored prayer flags, which mark spots of holiness, and after adding a handful of barley flour to it and some wine, they set it on fire, silently praying. Smoke curls up all day along the river. Similar fires are burned on the hilltops above the river, for this is the day not only to do homage to deities of the river and plain but also to those of the hills and mountains. When the prayer is over, each family party forms a semicircle before the fire, and with a handful of barley flour they cheer three times in unison, "*Ki Ki So So,*" and then shout, "*Lha Gye!*"* tossing the flour into the air. Now that the dedication is over and everyone is happy, people start looking for a shady spot.

All know by heart every inch of the groves, and each party has its favorite haunt. The picnickers spread their carpets and empty their food baskets. The contents are simple, comprising barley flour, butter, tea, dried meat, cheese, dried almonds, candies, and an abundant supply of the Tibetan wine, Ch'ang. Men, women, and children alike help themselves heartily to the cooling intoxicant. Without Ch'ang a Tibetan never becomes really merry.

To protect themselves against the sun or the scrutiny of passing crowds, some parties bring along a one-piece cloth shelter which they tie on the trees, while others put up rough muslin screens. For amusement they have Tibetan cards, mah-jongg, dice, musical instruments, and archery equipment. The popular Tibetan dice game, in which two to four people take part, is an energetic one. The players put two dice in a covered wooden bowl, which they shake onto a leather cushion with a heavy thump and a shout. The points determine the movement of the player's marks in a race, and the winner collects all the forfeits.

The Tibetan music played here is sweet and graceful, all of it suitable for singing and dancing. The people from Kham are famous marathon dancers. Joining in a circle, men and women with arms around each other's

* *Lha Gye* means "Victory to God," while the meaning of *Ki Ki So So,* said to be of Bon Po origin, seems to have been lost.

shoulders go on singing questions and answers and dancing for hours at a time. Flirtation is abundant. Young blades in high boots and cocked hats chase after smart, giggling girls. Women in dazzling costumes parade along, courting public attention. Visits are paid and returned, and food exchanged. Beggars and dogs swarm about.

The well-to-do exhibit their best tents, crowding certain spots till it is like a bazaar. These tent dwellers do not come for a day, but settle down for a week, a fortnight, or even longer. Servants are busy fetching water, cooking, stirring tea at the wooden churn, and chattering to their neighbors in the next tent. Inside the tents, parties or games are going on with much laughter. Glutted with food and drink, the more indolent ones sally out in quest of a quiet corner where they may loosen their belts and tumble into a heap amid their voluminous clothes, to doze the whole afternoon.

The women have their gambols in the river. They climb down to the sandbanks with baskets of washing. When the sun is tempting and the stream not icy cold, they take their clothes off. In loose petticoats they wade half nude into the shallow stream to swim, while their clothes are spread out on the sand to dry. The long sandbanks, submerged only in the rainy season, then wear the look of a beach.

When the sun is down and the moon is up, the greater part of the reveling public pour back into town, a boisterous crowd, but certainly one of the merriest in the world. Men and women arm in arm walk on unsteady legs, singing and laughing like children. We shall never forget a scene we saw on one of these occasions. Amid a noisy crowd an old man was following an old dame, probably his wife, both much under the effect of Ch'ang. The man held the end of a yak-hair rope like a whip, with which at every few steps he angrily gave a resounding whack on his companion's buttocks. At each stroke he cursed, she laughed, and the crowd cheered. We never found out what the matter was, but we were sure that both the performers and the spectators were enjoying a prodigious joke.

## Opera Season in the Forbidden Jewel Park

From the beginning to the middle of the seventh Tibetan month, opera season is in full swing in Lhasa. But, somewhat irrelevantly, the season is known as Zho-Ton (the handing out of sour milk). The name originates from a service in Dre-Pung monastery on the last day of the sixth month, when the outgoing chief proctors hand over authority to their successors; the latter, in keeping with an old tradition, used to treat the whole congregation to sour milk. Nowadays, because of the growth of the Dre-Pung congregation, only a small quantity of Zho is apportioned to the assembly in the great prayer hall. But the Zho-Ton celebration has, since the rise of Dre-Pung and the Dalai Lama, usurped both the name and significance of the original service.

The Zho-Ton is now a festival for all Lhasa, and the best dramatic talents of Tibet, mostly from Tsang, are represented. Troupes which are to take part in the celebration as a part of their obligation, or Khrai, must report for duty at Dre-Pung on the thirtieth day of the sixth month and give an informal performance in the monastery. The next day they give a dress rehearsal at the Potala and another at Nor-Bu Ling-Ka, formally marking the beginning of the opera season. For the following four or five days, the Dalai Lama entertains his whole court with the best plays by the best troupes in Tibet, and a part of the forbidden precincts of the Jewel Park is thrown open to the public.

A Tibetan theater, an open-air affair, has no stage. It is surrounded on all sides by the audience. A pair of musicians mark the spot where the modern backdrop should be, while actors walk in and out from amid the crowd. For some unknown reason, Tibetans call their actors *A-Cha Lha-Mo* (sister goddesses). Possibly this name arises from the fame of a certain actor or actress in playing the part of a goddess. No one seems to know the origin of the Tibetan theater. Competent opinions attribute the invention to the ascetic Thang-Tung Gye-Po, the bridge builder of the fifteenth century, with Chinese influences in a later stage. All players, professional or amateur, now worship him as their patron god.

The repertory of the Tibetan stage is severely limited. Taken altogether, there are not more than a dozen plays, of which only seven or eight are popular. With few exceptions, all the troupes are amateur, each specializing in only one or two plays. Four troupes are selected for the rare honor of playing before the Dalai and his court at this time of the year. They comprise either monks or farmers, who come as a duty. Those who do not play properly get flogged afterward. Women also play leading roles, though not in the lama troupes. They are banned in Nor-Bu Ling-Ka, where women's roles are played by men using their masculine voices.

The theater at Nor-Bu Ling-Ka is a stone-paved courtyard about one hundred twenty by ninety feet in size, covered by a huge tent. At the longer end is a two-story pavilion. From its upper floor, the Dalai Lama and the regent watch the show from behind a curtain of yellow gauze. The two sides of the theater are reserved for officials of both the ecclesiastical and the secular courts. All in uniform, they are seated on low cushions or carpets, according to precedence. Only the lower end is for the public, but even there the best seating space, near the stage, is reserved for the families of the nobility, in which the ladies, with their angular and fantastically rich headdresses, are especially prominent. The masses stand around, jostling and pushing, and occasionally get whipped. Since the same plays are given every year by the same troupes, many come not for the show but for a picnic in the Dalai's garden. They find it hard to stay away. A Lhasa festival without them would be unthinkable.

Before the play starts, a prologue is sung by a choir, usually of eight persons, wearing flat masks with flowing white hair, broad-sleeved coats, and netlike aprons of yak hair with a few rounded tassels on them. Holding horse-whips with colored tufts, they sing of the glory of Buddha and his triumphs, for an appropriate beginning. Then the actors troop in severally, forming a circle to the music of a drum and a pair of cymbals, and the play begins.

The drum used on a Tibetan stage, like that seen in the monasteries, is about two feet in diameter and stands on a tall pedestal. The musician squats on the ground, holding it with one hand, and beats it with a curved metal striker somewhat like a scythe. The leader seems to be the cymbal player, by whose clanking one is able to tell whether a particular actor is already on the stage or off it.

A play would be a boring affair if the players should remain stationary in a circle, especially when one remembers that a Tibetan play lasts at least a full day without intermission. The actors vary their parts with recitation, singing, and dialogue. Recitation is done by one, or by several in turn, in a loud monotonous tone, while everyone else on the stage stands still. The recitation gives the background of the action about to take place and conveniently fills up gaps between scenes. The singing, which sounds as simple as it is difficult, is led by the chief actor at a sustained high pitch, and after a sort of yodeling the others join in, making a din which can be heard at least a half mile away. No musical instrument can possibly accompany such vocal strainings. And it is just as well. For as the day draws on and the singers get hoarse, they drop the pitch, note by note, to suit their own convenience.

After the singing or recitation, the cymbal and drum pick up again, and the players start a kind of dance, moving back and forth in position. When interest is lagging, they move around the circle or start spinning round and round, with their apronlike pants ballooning like ballet skirts.

Very few people seem to understand the text of the singing and recitation, so the dialogue—in the vernacular—supplies welcome relief. But most welcome are the clowns; every Tibetan play has at least a few of them. A clown is the freest and happiest improviser, introducing abundant incidents and jokes of current interest. When a couple of clowns start their antics, they afford not only comic relief to the play but physical relief to the other actors, who squat on the ground to rest.

Since all plots are built on Buddhist lore, most of the plays have their background in old India. The hero or heroine is always an Indian prince or princess, and many villains are Brahmins. Virtue inevitably triumphs over evil, and hard trials culminate in happy endings. There are two well-known exceptions. One is a historical play about the marriage of King Son-Tsan Gam-Po to the Chinese and Nepalese princesses; the other is a touching tale about a pious Tibetan girl, born of humble stock in Gyantse. In all the happy endings may be found represented a kind of Tibetan equivalent of the United Nations ideal with Chinese, Indians, Nepalese, Bhutanese, Ladakhese, and Mohammedans (regarded by the Tibetans as a special group, who come mostly from Chinghai, with a few from Chinese Turkestan and India). Some props are used in Tibetan plays; costumes are crude; acting is to be interpreted with the widest latitude; and anachronism is most complete.

For four or five days, Tibetan officials hurry to the theater every morning to attend the show. They return late in the evening. The road to Nor-Bu Ling-Ka is full of people going to or from the opera. Traffic becomes especially congested in the evening when the crowd swarms back, singing, "*A-Cha Lha-Ma*"* at the top of their voices and making the words echo throughout the city.

The troupes, having wound up their official performance at Nor-Bu Ling-Ka, give private shows at the leading monasteries and noble houses in town. A-Cha Lha-Mo remains the talk of Lhasa for another ten days. After that, any further performance is banned until the next year.

To the most popular opera troupe certain beliefs are attached. Once the best actors of Tibet came from the ancient Me-Ru monastery in Lhasa. Many of them, it is said, were such expert actors that they became professionals; others mingled freely with women. The guardian deity of the monastery was angered, and consequently the Me-Ru troupe is now allowed to perform only once in about twelve years, or by special order of the government. Other acting groups are forbidden to overstay the period of Zho-Ton, since they might otherwise corrupt the morals of both the priests and the lay community.

* Originally the term for "actor," but now also meaning the play, and even the songs in the play; hence, it is almost identical to the opera.

# The Turn of the Seasons

Something has already been said about the women of Lhasa bathing in the river during the picnic season. There is also a period of about one week, fixed every year by the astrologers, when bathing in the mountain streams is believed to ensure good health. This week falls in either the seventh or the eighth month, when the star Ri-Shi makes its annual appearance and sheds its purifying light on all the rivers. Then both commoners and noblemen bathe in the Water of Pleasure. Tents are put up on the banks, and men, women, and children give themselves a thorough scrubbing in the chilly stream.

This week of bathing marks the end of the Ling-Ka, or picnicking time. Trees begin to shed their leaves and the meadows show the first tinges of brown. With the warm months over, the coming of the cold season is heralded some time in the ninth month by the return in state of the Dalai Lama to his winter quarters at the Potala.

The passing of the warm season also means the passing of the rainy season. The people throughout Tibet begin to whitewash the exteriors of their houses, white being the color of prosperity. In Lhasa, the signal is given by the Potala. When bucketful after bucketful of lime water is dashed over its white façade, all the households in town follow suit. By the same simple process, a three-story building gets whitewashed within an hour.

This yearly whitewashing, according to one story, is undertaken to please the eyes of a patron goddess who makes her annual round of Lhasa on the fifteenth day of the tenth month. Many legends have been spun about this goddess, Pai Lha Mo, and her associates, but probably not many in Lhasa know exactly who she is. Among the many famous images in the Central Cathedral is a fierce representation of the goddess, the face being formed of a single piece of stone, to which a wooden body was added later, but without a left arm. As she is the recognized patroness of Me-Ru monastery, the image is assigned to the care of the monks from that monastery. Every year the painted features on the stone face are washed off and repainted, and on the fifteenth day of the tenth month the image is borne by a monk from Me-Ru in a procession once around the town. Wine and white scarves are offered by the populace wherever the procession passes. It is believed that the bearer of the image can tell from the weight of his burden what is going to befall Tibet in the forthcoming year.

Ten days later comes the anniversary of the death of Tson-Kha-Pa, the founder of the Ge-Lu-Pa sect. Prayers are offered all over Tibet by the Ge-Lu monasteries, and especially at Gan-Dan, founded by the reformer himself. In the morning, monastic and lay officers ride in summer garments from Lhasa to a ceremony in the Potala and return in their winter uniforms.

But the great event of this anniversary is the display of oil lamps at night. As soon as darkness descends, thousands of tiny flickering lights illuminate the roofs and windows of all the houses in town. The scene of the great monasteries, their terraces adorned with innumerable oil lamps, and with trumpets and clarinets calling in the evening service, brings a religious fervor to many pious hearts. In the dim light people are seen hurrying about from lamp to lamp to add fresh oil. A pyre of the scented herb, *Sang*, sputters and sends forth its pale blue smoke from every roof, filling the night air with a rich aroma. Men and women with folded hands keep mumbling, "Praise to Tson-Kha-Pa, the leading thinker of the Land of Snow." The same night, within the Central Cathedral, the last of the three yearly initiation ceremonies for government officers is held under the chairmanship of the four cabinet ministers.

After the night of the lamp offerings, outdoor life becomes out of season. People look ahead to the year's end with little to enliven the intervening days. There is one minor festival marking the beginning of the eleventh month. Its exact date varies every year according to astrological determinations. It is not a festival, really, but a superstition, as some Tibetans themselves call it, bearing the queer name of the "Assembly of Nine Bad Lucks." It occurs for half a day on two separate days. When the time comes, the people of Lhasa desist from all serious business. Even government offices are closed down. However, the ingenious bridge builder, Thang-Tung Gye-Po, was born on one of these unlucky days and neutralized it by re-naming it the "Assembly of Nine Good Lucks." Tibetans have since made it an occasion for drinking of Ch'ang and merriment.

## New Year Pageantry

In the latter half of the Tibetan twelfth month, the southern suburb of Lhasa begins humming with activity. Conscript workers, including both men and women, troop in long files, each bearing bundles of fuel and chanting in unison under the surveillance of a whip-wielding petty officer. They bring fuel for use during the New Year prayer, when about twenty thousand monks assemble in Lhasa. More workers are busy leveling the four flagpoles in the main street, Bar-Kor, to mend them and to put on new prayer flags. Houses put up new strips of red and white cloth above their windows and doors.

Prayer flags and canopies, which adorn the housetops, must all be renewed. Housewives begin frying flour cakes, heaps of them, in butter or vegetable oil, to be exchanged as New Year gifts among friends and relatives. When the year draws near its end, houses are dusted and new *Thang Ka* (painted scrolls) are hung in the family chapels, where guests are expected. Then, before every altar are displayed pyramids of the fried cakes; *Dro-Ma*, a tiny root which is an indispensable item on all auspicious occasions; and a complete set of articles, comprising a pot of wine, an empty silver bowl, one wooden tray of barley flour, and another of wheat grains, on both of which are stuck straws and butter sticks and a kind of red wild flower called "New Year flower."

To various classes of Tibetans, the New Year comes at different times. In the first half of the twelfth month the farmers begin their celebration; in the second half the monasteries observe their holidays; and then the New Year itself arrives, leaving in its wake a crowded program of the celebrations and pageants which every Tibetan cherishes.

Tibetans are great lovers of show. They have a name for it—*Te-Mo*, which may mean anything from a street fight to a state procession. The first event to mark the beginning of the great season of Te-Mo is the "Devil's Dance" at the Potala on the twenty-ninth day of the last month.

This event takes place in a spacious stone courtyard in the east wing of the Potala. Accompanied by a picturesque lama band of drummers and trumpeters under the direction of a cymbal player, about fifty elaborately dressed actors take part in a solemn liturgic drama concerning the chastisement of evil spirits by the guardian deities of Buddhism and the black-hatted priests. The climax of the show comes when the leading priest tosses a cupful of wine onto a picture of a demon in a boiling pot of oil, which is then lighted and shoots high into the air in a column of flame and smoke. The performers are from the Dalai's private church, and the masks and costumes are said to be ordered from Peking.

The same service is organized by almost every monastery throughout Tibet. In households, a similar though much simpler ceremony takes place. One man carries a plateful of the boiled barley flour with vegetable dressings and brandishes a bundle of sticks, while another follows with a burning torch. They run from room to room shouting, "Away, away with you devils!" and then dump their loads out of the door, shooting their firearms or setting off a firecracker.

On New Year's Eve, auspicious signs, such as the swastika, the flower vase, flowers, the sun, and the moon, are painted in white on walls, pillars, and beams, and also on the ground in front of doors. Each family sits down

*Headman of a tribe in eastern Tibet dressed to attend a state function.*

*A dance of the women of Kham*

173

*Tibetan maidens*

*A bevy of Lhasa socialites*

*A Tibetan bride with her maids of honor and servants*

*Tidy corner
of a family altar.*

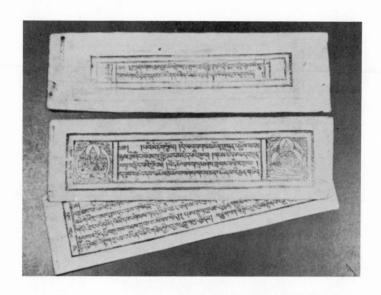

*Pages from the life of the thirteenth Dalai Lama.*
*A Tibetan book is composed of unbound leaves, with the letters*
*printed from wooden blocks. (Courtesy of C. T. Hu.)*

*The Simla Conference of 1913 was held under British leadership. In the center,*
*seated: Sir Henry McMahon, Secretary for External Affairs, the Government of India.*
*Standing behind him are Mr. Archibald Rose and Sir Charles Bell. Seated, from the*
*left: the Chinese Representative, the Maharaja of Sikkim, Mr. Ivan Chen, McMahon,*
*Tibetan delegates Lon-Chen Shatra and Tre-Men, and a member of the Chinese suite.*

Letter from the ninth
Panchen Lama to An-Chin
Hutukhtu. The seal at the end
of the writing (it is applied with
red ink) is used only by a
high incarnation lama.
(Courtesy of C. J. Hu.)

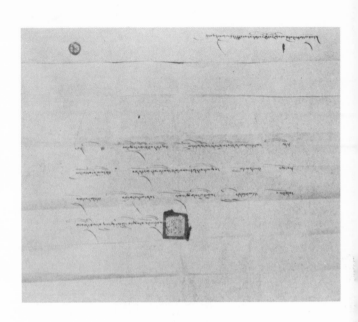

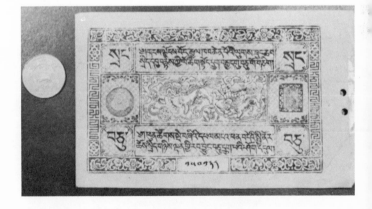

Tibet has its own currency. The gold coin is one of a
few coined before the government mint was destroyed
by fire. The seals in the middle row of the paper note are
those of the Dalai Lama and the Ka-Sha (cabinet). The holes
at the right side are for tying notes with string.

*Author*
*Tsung-lien*
*Shen (left)*
*and Sur-Kang Dsa-Sa, chief of the*
*Tibetan Bureau for External Affairs.*

A seventeen-point agreement between Communist China and Tibet was signed on
May 23, 1951, in the former Imperial Palace at Peking. Signing the pact are
(from right) chief delegate of the Central People's government Li Wei-han,
delegates Chang Ching-wu (now political representative of Communist China in
Tibet), Chang Kuo-hua (commander of the Tibetan garrison army), and Sun Chih-yuan.
Standing (from right): Vice-Chairman Li Chi-shen, Commander-in-Chief Chu Teh,
Vice-Premier Chen Yun of Communist China, and Tibetan delegates Nga-Bou
Nga-Wang Jig-Me (leader), Khe-Mey So-Nan Wang-Di, and Thup-Ten Ten-Thar.

Chairman Mao Tse-tung entertains Tibetan
delegation leader Nga-Bou (left) and the
Panchen Lama (right) after the conclusion
of the Sino-Tibetan Agreement.

Chi-Ch'u (*Water of Pleasure*) meanders through
the southern suburbs of Lhasa. The Chi-Ch'u valley is
the cultural center of modern Tibet.

to a simple dinner—simple because there is much to do. Everyone wants to be the first to arrive in the Central Cathedral. A huge crowd keeps a vigil outside its gate. As soon as its heavy doors swing open at midnight, the crowd rushes into every temple, where the images have been decked out in new clothes and the butter lamps lighted. Out in the night, passing from door to door, can be heard the clamor of masked singers, who sing glibly of good fortune to every family that presents them with scarves, wine, fried cakes, and money. When New Year's Eve draws to its end, every street resounds with galloping horses as government officers in their New Year's clothing hurry off for the morning audience at the Potala.

For the next three days, Lhasa suspends all business to observe the New Year. There is a ceremony each morning at the Potala. The first is in honor of the Dalai Lama as the religious leader; the second is in honor of him as the political leader; and the third is in honor of him as Tibet's guardian of Buddhism. We have described in detail in a previous chapter the proceedings at the first ceremony. The ceremony on the next day follows very much the same pattern, except that the secular court is more prominent and the first initiation service for the new government officers is observed.

Another interesting event marks the second ceremony. A high pole is erected below the Potala, and a picked man from the district of Tsang climbs up to a revolving plank at its top to do a few antics to amuse the crowd. The older generation recalls that in earlier days, in the time of the Thirteenth Dalai Lama, the man used to glide down a rope on a wooden saddle fastened to another rope suspended from the top of the central portion of the Potala to its base, a height of three hundred feet. So many died from falling off or being burned as the saddle caught fire due to friction with the rope that the Thirteenth Dalai discontinued the event and substituted the present one. It is said that when the people of Tsang were pressed into service to expand the Potala to its present form in the time of the Fifth Dalai Lama, they built the Red Palace in such a way that its upper portion was larger than the lower, thus representing an inverted pagoda. The regent, Sang-Gye Gyam-Tsho, thereupon imposed on them a punishment. Every year a native from Tsang was to make a dangerous descent from the top of the Red Palace on behalf of them all.

On the third day of the New Year, the last and most important flagpole in Lhasa is raised. This is the pole that stands guard over Tibet's political fate. Both magistrates of Lhasa are present to supervise the job. As soon as it is completed, the magistrates hurry on horseback to the Potala to report the affair to the Dalai. Then and only then the ceremony begins in honor of the Dalai Lama as guardian of Buddhist religion.

On the same day, the monks from Dre-Pung, Se-Ra, and Gan-Dan monasteries converge on Lhasa, doubling its population. There are dormitories for each monastery in Lhasa where the monks are billeted. Lanes and streets begin to swarm with a crop-haired, maroon-clad mob. Now begins the greatest of all festivals in Tibet, *Mon-Lam Ch'en-Po*, the Great Prayer.

## The Great Prayer

The third day of the Tibetan New Year is the beginning of the Great Prayer. The event begins with an uproar. Lhasa is on the alert for the coming of the proctors of Dre-Pung with their retinue of lama ruffians. At some time before noon, the proctors, wearing their finest garments, sweep down on the town like conquerors, riding on ponies bedecked with clanging bells. The ruffians shout their approach and scold pedestrians off, left and right. After riding once in pomp around Bar-Kor (streets in the Middle Circle), they dismount at a corner of the Central Cathedral to set up their headquarters as the wardens of Lhasa during the following twenty-one days.

By a special edict of the Fifth Dalai Lama, the proctors of Dre-Pung, his alma mater, were made wardens of public security for Lhasa during the whole period of the Great Prayer. A most interesting ceremony marks their assumption of duty. As soon as the proctors are installed in office, two deputies are appointed who are dressed exactly like the proctors, complete with iron rod, the emblem of authority, to make a proclamation to the public. Heralded by their muscular henchmen, who are armed with whips and poles and have faces smeared with soot, the two deputies march to the front of the magistrate's headquarters. The door of the headquarters is closed, its police force having been previously withdrawn. Twelve members of the staff, standing four abreast, hat in hand, bow low behind a smoking pyre, ready to attend on the lamas. The two deputies sally forth in turn, each to deliver in a most pompous and dramatic manner a sonorous lecture, reminding the staff of the assumption of dictatorial power by the proctors of Dre-Pung during the Great Prayer and warning the secular population, including the nobility, to behave. After completion of the speeches, the staff of the magistrate's headquarters hurriedly lock up their office and scatter until authority is returned to them at the end of the Great Prayer period. The deputies march north to a spring, where they deliver another speech, exhorting the dragon spirit not to fail to supply water during this important period. A third speech, an order of banishment, is given to a representative from the city temple of the deity Ka-Ma-Sha, the oracle of Se-Ra monastery. A fourth speech at another spring winds up this part of the affair.

The following story about Ka-Ma-Sha throws interesting sidelights on the rivalry between the Dre-Pung and Se-Ra monasteries. Before the days of the Fifth Dalai Lama, it is said, the authority for maintaining peace and order in Lhasa during the Great Prayer was entrusted by turns to the proctors of both monasteries. The Ka-Ma-Sha oracle then enjoyed as revered a position as Nai-Ch'ung, the oracle of Dre-Pung. One year when Se-Ra was in charge, as the story goes, Ka-Ma-Sha, being jealous of the rising importance of Dre-Pung, surreptitiously put poison into a container of tea for the Dre-Pung congregation. Hundreds of lives would certainly have been lost had not their oracle, Nai-Ch'ung, suddenly seized with a premonition, hurled a knife from Dre-Pung monastery to Lhasa, wounding one leg of the murderous deity, Ka-Ma-Sha. A scarred pillar in the Central Cathedral still bears evidence of the story. Nai-Ch'ung saved the day, and since then not only have the proctors of Dre-Pung been made the sole wardens of peace and order for the Great Prayer, but Ka-Ma-Sha is to be expelled from Lhasa every year during the Great Prayer to prevent further mischief.

Those who run the Great Prayer gain much money. In the name of religion the two proctors collect taxes on business, livestock, and amusements, and levy penalties against which there is no appeal. Twice a day scouting parties are sent out to inspect the "hygienic conditions" in the city. Those who are found guilty of neglect are given corporeal punishment on the spot, to be avoided only by the payment of a fine. Indeed, seldom does a proctor return to Dre-Pung after the Great Prayer without having become a rich lama.

Beginning on the fourth day of the New Year, there are six services each day, of which three are "wet"—that is, with tea—and three are "dry." The first service in the morning is presided over by Gan-Dan Khri-Pa, the pope of Ge-Lu-Pa. During the three "dry" services, the first-class doctors of divinity debate publicly against any challenger. After the three "wet" services, alms are distributed to the congregation at the various doors of the Central Cathedral.

Almsgiving during the Great Prayer is considered an especially effective means of gaining merits. Among such a large congregation, the Tibetans reason, there must be a good sprinkling of Arhans, Asuras, and other intermediaries between Buddha and men, for whom it will be a privilege to do good. A huge fund, created by a special endowment from the Chinese emperors in Manchu times, is in operation, the interest from which is doled out at this time of the year to the monks of the Three Seats, the two Tantric academies, and to a few monks from other monasteries. The office entrusted with the management of this fund is known as the "Office of the Lama's Steward." It is to this office that every prospective patron must apply for setting the day and hour of giving alms to the congregation. One may also entrust the distribution to this office. How much of the interest from the fund actually goes to charity may be guessed from the fact that many destitute monks derive their main support from it.

The first important festival after the Great Prayer gets under way is the butter lamp offerings on the fifteenth day of the month. Early in the morning, wooden scaffoldings, rising three stories high, line the inside of Bar-Kor like derricks in an oil field. Toward evening, frames of pictures inlaid in colored butter, with all the auspicious figures and designs, are rigged up on the derricks, turning the street into an open gallery of lamaist art. As soon as night descends, the gallery is illuminated by butter lamps and gas lights from below. The Dalai and his whole court are the first to be invited to make the rounds amid music and lanterns. Then the people follow in a surging tide. It is said that this festival originated with a dream of the Great Fifth Dalai Lama, who might have borrowed the idea from the Chinese lantern festival of the year's first full moon. The dream was of many beautiful and auspicious scenes in a Buddhist wonderland, which he wished to commemorate by re-enacting it on the same night each year.

The best exhibition of plastic art in lamadom is to be seen at Tson-Kha-Pa's birthplace, the Kum-Bum monastery at Chinghai, where artists work for months in order to produce one night's extravaganza. But whether at Kum-Bum or Lhasa, the whole display, like a dream, is gone before daybreak. Nothing must remain of so much splendor and beauty when the first shaft of sun reaches the scene, in order to drive home the Buddhist theme that life is transitory and has no more substance than dreams.

For six days in succession, from the twenty-second day of the first month, there is a spectacle every day for the people of Lhasa. The secular arm of the Dalai's court joins in the jubilation. Two lay officers are appointed commanders to head an army of medieval knights levied from the noble families and the older government offices as a part of their Khrai duty. This cavalry foray comes into existence to wage a phantom war against the potential enemies of Buddhism. The participants look as fantastic as their mission is professed to be. Dressed in suits of mail armor with plumed helmets, and armed with beflagged spears, bows and arrows, and firelock guns, they ride on coursers as gaily bedecked as themselves. On the first day, the two commanders, having encamped at the open ground below the Potala, ride with their followers in rich ancient Chinese costumes to the Central Cathedral to receive instructions from the Dre-Pung proctors. On return to their camp, where they issue orders for the morrow, they are served wine by glamorous wine maids and silk-clad attendants.

The next morning, the cavalry, about one thousand strong and divided into left and right wings, are led by the commanders through the northern sand dunes to the plain north of Lhasa, where a small colony of tents has sprung up the previous night. A short review of the army takes place. The four ministers and the high lay officers are seated before a row of tents, and across from them a table of offerings is placed, flanked by two mounted standard bearers in steel armor. These bearers represent the war gods of Tibet (Red and Black Protectors). Four students from the finance school, dressed in uniforms with saucer caps, stand some distance from the minister's camp. Beginning with the right wing, an announcer calls unit after unit to the reviewing ground. As each unit files in, the four students, advancing toward the ministers and bowing low, announce in a crisp chanting tone that they have checked the number of men and horses, the condition of the armor and arms, and found all in order. The unit then rides off and the next is reviewed. The quaint costumes, the jerky movements of the principal actors, and the mechanical repetition of every detail suggest a puppet show.

But the greatest spectacle of all is reserved for the next day, the last day of the Great Prayer. Starting in early morning, the cavalry, reinforced by hundreds of foot soldiers—the old guard of the Dalai Lama—literally blast their way into Lhasa: the foot soldiers, also in mail armor and with helmets bedecked with flags and plumes, advance with shields and broadswords between two columns of their comrades, who keep firing their guns at every few steps, making a terrific din. The vanguard advances, with the cavalry following, until it invades the Bar-Kor. There the two commanders hold court in the open. Seated on an improvised dais, they receive heaps of scarves, for they are starting on a holy war, and all their friends have come to wish them victory.

After a short rest, the two commanders, with their aides-de-camp, walk up to the gate of the Central Cathedral to prostrate themselves before the Dalai Lama. The foot soldiers also march there to perform an ancient war dance. Then, led by the commanders and their aides, and amid guns and shouts, the whole cavalry rides past in formation to make one round of the Bar-Kor.

Inside the cathedral, two services are being held by the monks of Nam-Gye, the Dalai Lama's private church, and the Tantric school of Dre-Pung. The services, called *Jor-Gya*, of which Tibetans seem never to have enough, are for the chastisement of devils. Toward the end of the services, two columns of monks, each monk holding a drum, emerge from different doors of the cathedral followed by their Khen-Po, or president, who plays the cymbals. After each column come men carrying a huge effigy of a skull, raised on a stand that is painted with designs suggesting a burning pyre. The Khen-Po executes a mystic dance before the skull effigy. Then, preceded by scores of big banners, each representing a divinity, the two columns merge into one to proceed to the southern suburb. After them comes the oracle Nai-Ch'ung in a trance, his attendants, and the Gan-Dan Khri-Pa with the sixteen first-class doctors of divinity. On coming within sight of the suburb, where two pyres are standing, Nai-Ch'ung shoots an arrow in the direction of the pyres. His trance is now over. He faints, and is hurriedly borne back on a sedan chair. The pyres are immediately lighted and the skull effigy thrown into the fire amid volleys of shots by the foot soldiers. On the Ling-Kor two old cannons boom three times across the river toward a hill where a black tent stands with a black sheep, symbol of a demon, chained inside. Simultaneous with the cannonading, the two commanders and their thousand knights converge on the scene of the pyres. The effigy has been burned and the enemy is routed. Turning, they hastily circle the Bar-Kor once, amid shouts and cheers, and spread to the public news of the defeat of Buddha's enemies. The drama ends.

But not the celebrations. Now that the enemy is defeated and the world saved for Buddhism, a procession starts at dawn the next day to herald the coming of the next Buddha, whose image is drawn once around the Bar-Kor on a buffalo cart. Then follows great rejoicing, with competitions in wrestling, weight lifting, foot races, and horse races. When the celebration is over, the twenty thousand monks wind up their last prayer and disperse with the proctors of Dre-Pung, leaving Lhasa once more to its old order.

The lay festivities last two more days after this. The commanders and the cavalrymen assemble the next day north of the Potala to exhibit their horsemanship and skill in archery before the lay officers. Along a runway about three hundred feet long two targets are set up ninety feet from each other. A horseman, coming from one end at a gallop, fires at the first target with his firelock gun and, hastily strapping the gun on his shoulder, takes out his bow and arrow to hit the second target. The next day's program begins with a distance-shooting competition by certain selected archers. Then all the lay officers join in a target-shooting competition, which ends with wine and song.

Although this celebration of the Great Prayer was instituted by the reformer Tson-Kha-Pa himself, the lay festivities were no doubt added later by the Mongols, as Mongolian influence in dress, etiquette, and style of wrestling is evident.

# The Lesser Service

A Tibetan pundit told us that the Great Prayer, which had its remote origin in old India, was in memory of Sakya Muni's conquest of all heretics. The service used to last fifteen days until Tson-Kha-Pa added new significance to it and extended it to twenty-one. The Buddhists believe that the admittance of women, the lower beings, by Sakya Muni to his discipleship has cut short the life of Buddhism by five hundred years. So Tson-Kha-Pa, after seeing to the founding of the Three Seats of the Ge-Lu-Pa sect, dedicated a crown to Sakya Muni in the Central Cathedral and extended the observance of the Great Prayer with the wish to restore the five hundred years' loss.

About twenty days intervene between the end of the Great Prayer and the Lesser Service. This service, called *Tshom-Ch'o* (the Assembly Service), which is a smaller version of the Great Prayer, was organized by the famous regent Sang-Gye Gyam-Tsho in memory of the Fifth Dalai Lama. Beginning on the nineteenth day of the second month, it lasts twelve days. The day before it begins, the proctors of Dre-Pung once more ride in triumph to Lhasa. The same proclamations are made and the same services are held as during the Great Prayer, though with fewer lamas participating. The doctors of divinity, who sit through the public debates of this Lesser Service, are second-class doctors of divinity. There is one important change. Whereas Gan-Dan Khri-Pa, the pope of the Ge-Lu-Pa, plays the role of a patron in the Great Prayer—as the founder of the sect, Tson-Kha-Pa, did in his own life-time—he now joins in all prayers of the Lesser Service as one of the congregation.

The greatest event of the Lesser Service is again the chastisement of the evil spirit. But this time the demon to be chastised is said to be a historic figure. In the time of Khri-Son De-Tsan there lived one minister of state who was the incarnation of a devil. He has done much mischief not only in his lifetime but also afterward, having been reborn in the demonic world to persist in the destruction of Buddhism. In recent times, however, the name of this mischievous character has been spelled in another form, to suggest the meaning of a rebellious scapegoat. And instead of one, there are two such scapegoats each year for the occasion.

A few days before the Lesser Service starts, the two demons descend on Lhasa. They are ordinary Tibetans of flesh and blood coming in response to their Khrai duty. Dressed in plain clothing and a saucer cap, each has a page, who as a mark of identity bears a yellow cloth bundle on his back, holds a whip, and is followed by a white dog. The demons come to ask for "wine money" from door to door, and they are authorized to buy daily provisions in Lhasa at half price. Sometimes they bring along a bushy yak tail, an especially dreaded thing. It is believed that a mere flick of this tail at anybody is enough to bring bad luck to him for the rest of the year.

The full force of the older Tantric academy, Gyu-Me, is mobilized for chastising the scapegoats. For seven days the monks prepare their most venomous curse, passing around a human skull filled with wine, into which everyone spits until the day of chastisement. The wine, which is called the "Bewitched Water," is then administered to the two demons. These demons come on this day with their faces painted half black and half white, and dressed in sheepskins with hats bedecked with red flags. They hold in one hand a magic wand and in the other the dreaded yak's tail. Hung on one side of their bodies is a weighing scale and on the other a measuring cup, both symbolical of their power over the material world. Advancing to the Central Cathedral in a challenging manner, they dance and shout to all their demonic families to come to witness their gamble with Tibet. They challenge a priest of the Nying-Ma-Pa sect to throw dice to decide the fate of Tibet. If they win, they will have a free hand in Tibet; but if they lose, they agree to go away till the next year. The priest accepts the challenge, and the gambling takes place under the supervision of representatives of the Dalai Lama and the Tibetan government. In the old days, we are told, there was some attempt at honesty in the game. Yet the dice then used were no less fakes than they are today; for the priest used a die all six faces of which were marked with "6" spots, and the demons used one with all the faces marked with "1" spots. But both dice also bore the genuine spots on the corner of each face, enabling the overseers to submit a secret report on the true result of the contest. The Thirteenth Dalai, however, ordered the marks on the corners to be removed. Thus, since then, every time the demons come to renew their challenge, unqualified victory for the Nying-Ma-Pa priest is assured.

At the moment victory is won for Tibet, a procession starts from the Central Cathedral. It consists of the usual effigy and the monks of the Gyu-Me monastery; Nai-Ch'ung, the state oracle; and Gan-Dan Khri-Pa, pope of Ge-Lu-Pa sect; with the new doctors. In the southern suburb the effigy is burned on a pyre. Two stout lama ruffians, clutching the defeated demons by their collars, banish them from Lhasa, one to the southern suburb and the other to the northern. They must not be allowed once to turn their eyes back on the city. The crowds on the streets start clapping their hands, whistling, and spitting at the approach of the demons. Those with a more sensitive conscience throw them money wrapped in paper, along with some of their own fingernails, hair, or old clothes, thus inviting them to carry away their bad luck. All of these articles are dutifully collected by the servants

Tibet and the Tibetans

of the demons in their aprons. The demon in the south is banished to the Sam-Ye monastery and the one in the north to the valley of Phon-Po. They are supposed to have carried away all the potential misfortunes of Tibet for the year and are never to return. As a matter of fact, their exile does not last twenty-one days.

The Lesser Service ends in a great parade on the last day of the second month. At dawn a long colorful procession, unlike any previous one, issues from the Central Cathedral and slowly winds its way to the Potala. It is a parade of a Buddhist's spiritual and material wealth: umbrellas, canopies, incense burners, lanterns, flowers, sacred utensils for baptism, holy musical instruments, masked dancers, drummers, esoteric and exoteric monks, and elephants. It symbolizes the dedication of all his subjects to the Fifth Dalai Lama, as laid down in the writings of his loyal regent, Sang-Gye Gyam-Tso. When the front part of the mile-long procession reaches the Potala, a huge painted picture of the Buddhas, both present and future, which can be seen several miles off, is hung in front of the Potala by scores of men using improvised pulleys. The procession passes below the picture and returns north of the Potala to the Cathedral. This last ceremony is known as "the Hoistings of the Monks."

When the last event of the Lesser Service is over and the lamas disperse, Lhasa stirs in the warming breath of spring. The two services of the New Year fall during the worst time of the year, the season of dust storms. In fact, the people of Lhasa call these storms "the lama wind," because they come with the lamas. These storms are the unmistakable heralds of springtime. For when their fury is spent, toward the end of the Lesser Service, trees put out their first sprays of green and the fields become verdant again. The people of Lhasa relax in the warm air and, recalling how the New Year was appropriately and successfully observed, they agree that they have good reason to look ahead to another year of peace and prosperity.

# Official Text of the Agreement Signed in Peking on May 23, 1951, in the Former Imperial Palace

## The Agreement of the Central People's Government and the Local Government of Tibet on Measures for the Peaceful Liberation of Tibet

### PREAMBLE

The Tibetan nationality is one of the nationalities with a long history within the boundaries of China and, like many other nationalities, it has performed its glorious duty in the course of the creation and development of our great Motherland. But over the last one hundred years or more, imperialist forces penetrated into China, and in consequence also penetrated into the Tibetan region and carried out all kinds of deceptions and provocations. Like previous reactionary governments, the Kuomintang reactionary government continued to carry out a policy of oppressing and sowing dissension among the nationalities, causing division and disunity among the Tibetan people. And the local government of Tibet did not oppose the imperialist deceptions and provocations, and adopted an unpatriotic attitude toward our great Motherland. Under such conditions, the Tibetan nationality and people were plunged into the depths of enslavement and suffering.

In 1949, basic victory was achieved on a nation-wide scale in the Chinese People's War of Liberation; the common domestic enemy of all nationalities—the Kuomintang reactionary government—was overthrown; and the common foreign enemy of all the nationalities—the aggressive imperialist forces—was driven out. On this basis, the founding of the People's Republic of China and of the Central People's government was announced. In accordance with the Common Programme passed by the Chinese People's Political Consultative Conference, the Central People's government declared that all nationalities within the boundaries of the People's Republic of China are equal, and that they shall establish unity and mutual aid and oppose imperialism and their own public enemies, so that the People's Republic of China will become a big fraternal and co-operative family, composed of all its nationalities; that within the big family of all nationalities of the People's Republic of China, national regional autonomy shall be exercised in areas where national minorities are concentrated, and all national minorities shall have freedom to develop their spoken and written languages and to preserve or reform their customs, habits, and religious beliefs, while the Central People's government shall assist all national minorities to develop their political, economic, cultural, and educational construction work. Since then, all nationalities within the country, with the exception of those in the areas of Tibet and Taiwan, have gained liberation. Under the unified leadership of the Central People's government and the direct leadership of higher levels of People's government, all national minorities are fully enjoying the right of national equality and have established, or are establishing, national regional autonomy.

In order that the influences of aggressive imperialist forces in Tibet might be successfully eliminated, the unification of the territory and sovereignty of the People's Republic of China accomplished, and national defense safeguarded; in order that the Tibetan nationality and people might be freed and return to the big family of the People's Republic of China to enjoy the same rights of national equality as all the other nationalities in the country and develop their political, economic, cultural, and educational work, the Central People's government, when it ordered the People's Liberation Army to march into Tibet, notified the local government of Tibet to send delegates to the central authorities to conduct talks for the conclusion of an agreement on measures for the peaceful liberation of Tibet.

In the latter part of April 1951, the delegates with full powers of the local government of Tibet arrived in Peking. The Central People's government appointed representatives with full powers to conduct talks on a friendly basis with the delegates with full powers of the local government of Tibet. As a result of these talks, both parties agreed to conclude this agreement and guarantee that it will be carried into effect.

1. The Tibetan people shall unite and drive out imperialist aggressive forces from Tibet; the Tibetan people shall return to the big family of the Motherland—the People's Republic of China.

2. The local government of Tibet shall actively assist the People's Liberation Army to enter Tibet and consolidate the national defense.

3. In accordance with the policy toward nationalities laid down in the Common Programme of the Chinese People's Political Consultative Conference, the Tibetan people have the right of exercising national regional autonomy under the unified leadership of the Central People's government.

4. The central authorities will not alter the existing political system in Tibet. The central authorities also will not alter the established status, functions, and powers of the Dalai Lama. Officials of various ranks shall hold office as usual.

5. The established status, functions, and powers of the Panchen Ngoerhtehni shall be maintained.

6. By the established status, functions, and powers of the Dalai Lama and of the Panchen Ngoerhtehni are meant the status, functions, and powers of the Thirteenth Dalai Lama and of the Ninth Panchen Ngoerhtehni when they were in friendly and amicable relations with each other.

7. The policy of freedom of religious belief laid down in the Common Programme of the Chinese People's Political Consultative Conference shall be carried out. The religious beliefs, customs, and habits of the Tibetan people shall be respected, and lama monasteries shall be protected. The central authorities will not effect a change in the income of the monasteries.

8. Tibetan troops shall be reorganized by stages into the People's Liberation Army, and become a part of the national defense forces of the People's Republic of China.

9. The spoken and written language and school education of the Tibetan nationality shall be developed step by step in accordance with the actual conditions in Tibet.

10. Tibetan agriculture, livestock raising, industry, and commerce shall be developed step by step, and the people's livelihood shall be improved step by step in accordance with the actual conditions in Tibet.

11. In matters related to various reforms in Tibet, there will be no compulsion on the part of the central authorities. The local government of Tibet should carry out reforms of its own accord, and when the people raise demands for reform, they shall be settled by means of consultation with the leading personnel of Tibet.

12. In so far as former pro-imperialist and pro-Kuomintang officials resolutely sever relations with imperialism and the Kuomintang and do not engage in sabotage or resistance, they may continue to hold office irrespective of their past.

13. The People's Liberation Army entering Tibet shall abide by all the above-mentioned policies and shall also be fair in all buying and selling and shall not arbitrarily take a single needle or thread from the people.

14. The Central People's government shall conduct the centralized handling of all external affairs of the area of Tibet; and there will be peaceful co-existence with neighboring countries and establishment and development of fair commercial and trading relations with them on the basis of equality, mutual benefit, and mutual respect for territory and sovereignty.

15. In order to ensure the implementation of this agreement, the Central People's government shall set up a military and administrative committee and a military area headquarters in Tibet, and apart from the personnel sent there by the Central People's government shall absorb as many local Tibetan personnel as possible to take part in the work.

Local Tibetan personnel taking part in the military and administrative committee may include

*Tibet and the Tibetans*

patriotic elements from the local government of Tibet, various districts, and leading monasteries; the name list shall be drawn up after consultation between the representatives designated by the Central People's government and the various quarters concerned, and shall be submitted to the Central People's government for appointment.

16. Funds needed by the military and administrative committee, the military area headquarters, and the People's Liberation Army entering Tibet shall be provided by the Central People's government. The local government of Tibet will assist the People's Liberation Army in the purchase and transport of food, fodder, and other daily necessities.

17. This agreement shall come into force immediately after signatures and seals are affixed to it.

Signed and sealed by:
Delegates with full powers of the Central People's government:
Chief Delegate:
    Li Wei-han
Delegates:
    Chang Ching-wu
    Chang Kuo-hua
    Sun Chih-yuan
Delegates with full powers of the local government of Tibet:
Chief Delegate:
    Kaloon Ngabou Ngawang Jigme
Delegates:
    Dzasak Khemey Sonam Wangdi
    Khentrung Thupten Tenthar
    Khenchung Thupten Lekmuun
    Rimshi Samposey Tenzin Thundup

Peking, May 23, 1951.

# List of Books for Recommended Reading

BACOT, J. *Le Poète Tibetain Milarépa*. Editions Bossard. Paris, 1925.
———. *La Vie de Marpa*. Librairie Orientaliste. Paris: Paul Geuthner, 1937.
BELL, CHARLES. *The People of Tibet*. London: Oxford University Press, 1928.
———. *The Religion of Tibet*. London: Oxford University Press, 1931.
———. *Tibet, Past and Present*. London: Oxford University Press, 1924.
BURRARD, S., and HENRY HAYDEN. *Sketch of the Geography and Geology of the Himalayan Mountains and Tibet*. Survey of India. Dehra Dun, India, 1932–34.
DAS, S. C. *Journey to Lhasa and Central Tibet*. Edited by W. W. Rockhill. London: John Murray, 1902.
EVANS-WENTZ, W. Y. *The Tibetan Book of the Dead*. London: Oxford University Press, 1949.
FRANCKE, A. H. *Antiquities of Indian Tibet*. 2 vols. Calcutta: Superintendent Government Printing, 1914–26.
———. *A History of Western Tibet*. Partridge, 1907.
KAWAGUCHI, EKAI. *Three Years in Tibet*. Adyar, Madras: Vasanta Press, 1909.
KÖRÖS, ALEXANDER CSOMA, DE. *A Grammar of the Tibetan Language*. With Vaidurya dKarpo as Appendix. Calcutta, 1834.
HEDIN, S. *Trans-Himalaya*. 3 vols. London: The Macmillan Co., 1909–13.
HOLDICH, T. H. *Tibet the Mysterious*. London, 1905.
HUC, M. *Travels in Tartary, Tibet and China*. Chicago: Open Court Publishing Co., 1898.
OBERMILLER, E. *Bu-ston's History of Buddhism in India and Tibet*. Heidelberg: University of Heidelberg, 1932.
PETECH, L. *A Study on the Chronicles of Ladakh*. Calcutta: Calcutta Oriental Press, Ltd., 1939.
ROCKHILL, W. W. *The Dalai Lamas of Lhasa*. Leyden: Oriental Printing Office, 1910.
———. *The Land of the Lamas*. London: Longmans, Green, Ltd., 1891.
———. *The Life of Buddha*. London: Trubner's & Co., 1884.
ROERICH, G. N. *The Blue Annals*. Part I. Calcutta: Royal Asiatic Society of Bengal, 1949.
THOMAS, F. W. *Nam: An Ancient Language of the Sino-Tibetan Borderland*. London: Oxford University Press, 1948.
———. *Tibetan Literary Texts and Documents Concerning Chinese Turkestan*. Vol. I. London: The Royal Asiatic Society, 1935.
TRINKLER, E. *Tibet, Sein Geographisches Bild und Seine Stellung im Asiatischen Kontinent*. Univ. München, 1922.
TUCCI, G. *Indo-Tibetika*. 3 vols. Rome: Reale Accadèmia d'Italia, 1932–36.

# Index

*Tibet and the Tibetans*